Doctor D an Eastern Oregon Family Physician

Dorin S. Daniels, MD
1927-2022

So faith, hope, love abide, these three: but the greatest of these is love. 1 Corinthians 13: 13

Dorin S. Daniels, MD
Celebration of Life
February 5, 2022

Opening Prayer
Military Honors
Eulogy: Alan Daniels
Eulogy: Mike Daniels
Violin Solo: Emily Daniels
Scripture
Message: Danny Morrison
Closing Prayer

Pianist: Janet Morrison
Ushers: Tony, John, Matthew and Michael Daniels
Programs: Ayumi, Rachel, and Chelsey Daniels
Books: Megan and Ashley Daniels

(Family wearing bow ties that he wore in his practice)

Dorin Slater Daniels, MD, passed away Sunday, January 30, 2022, surrounded by loved ones. He was born on Sept. 23, 1927, in Madison, WI. His parents were Farrington Sr. and Olive Bell Daniels. He joined an older brother, Farrington, Jr., and two sisters, Florence, and Miriam. His father was a University of Wisconsin professor in physical chemistry and he grew up listening to the ideas of the scientists at the time. He went through high school in three years so he could join the Navy during World War II, and served as a Corpsman. After the war ended he went to Oberlin College. After graduation he took a job at the Oakridge Atomic Lab where he went to the island of Enewetak Atoll, and was involved in experiments testing the effects of atomic bomb radiation. He met his wife, Kathryn (Toddy) Meyer Daniels while working at Oakridge. They were married in Knoxville, TN, and were married over 50 years. They had 4 children, Don, Alan, Kathryn, and DeWilda. After that he was accepted to the University of Chicago School of Medicine. He spent the last 6 months of his college working as a surgeon for a doctor in a TB clinic in Alaska whose arthritic hands could no longer do surgery. He did his internship & residency at St. Vincent's Hospital in Portland, OR. He started his medical practice in Vale in 1958. After several years he realized he needed to be closer to the hospital and moved his family to Ontario, where he continued practicing. He delivered over 3500 babies in his career. He received many honors including being the Oregon Doctor of the Year in 1983 and receiving the President's Award for Outstanding Service in 1993. He retired in 1994 and continued as a Locum Tenens in several places. He and his wife also went on several Elder Hostel trips. He became involved in the Malheur Country Historical Society. He was president, was very involved in getting the Historical Society's books updated, and he helped video tape a lot of personal histories in the area and did a lot of the editing He was also involved in the Kiwanis, helping out wherever he could and taking pictures. He was the Winter Wonderland Grand Marshall in Dec. 2009, and the Ontario Chamber of Commerce Man of the year in Jan., 2015. He thoroughly enjoyed watching his kids, grandkids, and great-grandkids grow up.

Doctor D
an Eastern Oregon
Family Physician

By Dorin S. Daniels

ISBN 978-0-9824864-0-5

For Comments or Book Orders Contact:
DoctorDBook@gmailcom

Dorin S. Daniels
4457 Community Rd.
Ontario, OR 97914

This book is dedicated to my patients and family.

Table of Contents

Introduction VIII

Foreword IX

Chapter 01 – Childhood 1

Chapter 02 – Navy 23

Chapter 03 – College 31

Chapter 04 – Oak Ridge and Eniwetok 39

Chapter 05 – Medical School 49

Chapter 06 – Alaska 59

Chapter 07 – Portland – Internship and Residency 69

Chapter 08 – Vale – Starting Practice 75

Chapter 09 – Flying 95

Chapter 10 – Volunteering 101

Chapter 11 – Family Medicine – The Evolution of a Specialty 105

Chapter 12 – Ontario 109

Chapter 13 – Pregnant Ladies and Newborns 137

Chapter 14 – Health Planning 145

Chapter 15 – Education and Teaching 155

Chapter 16 – Retirement 163

Chapter 17 – Oops – Close Calls and Missed Headlines 171

Chapter 18 – Honors 177

Chapter 19 – The Future of Medicine – My Predictions 181

Afterword 187

COLOR PHOTO SECTION 189

Introduction

I never had a nickname that stuck throughout my childhood. In our family the name "Danny" was well established for my cousin Franc Jr. At one time or another, my brother, one sister and I acquired "Danny" as a nickname as did some other cousins. My sister Florence has been Danny to her husband and to her friends for most of her adult life. I was Danny for much of my time in the Navy and in college. My brother Farrington Jr. was Danny most of the time, especially after shedding his childhood nickname of Farry. My sister Miriam was Mino, except to a neighbor who called her "Miss Fish" – much to her annoyance. After I had my M.D. degree I became "Doc" to some, Doctor Dorin or Doctor Daniels to others, but gradually many of my office staff and closest associates and hospital nurses referred to me as "Doctor D". I always felt that Doctor D was used in an affectionate way and it has become the title for this, my first and probably only book.

Foreword

Many years ago, when I had small grandchildren, I made a proposed outline for a memoir that I thought I might eventually write. I moved that outline from one computer to the next, unchanged, as I upgraded to newer technologies. Recently when those young grandchildren were grown and had their own children they presented me with a small tape recorder and asked that I start recording my history so that they could inform their children about their great-grandfather. It still took me quite awhile to get started because I found it difficult to talk about "ME". I finally realized that my life was filled with some unique experiences that would be foreign to most people and that I had witnessed some changes in medicine which would not be generally known. While this writing is directed primarily toward my grandchildren and great-grandchildren I thought that there might be some elements of general interest concerning local and national medical history. I have taken the liberty of interjecting some thoughts about governmental intervention as well as some thoughts about where medicine may be going. I have had a good life. The bumps in the road along the way of life have been trivial compared to the joys I have experienced in working with my patients, colleagues, friends, and family over these many years.

Dorin S. Daniels, M.D. - retired
Ontario, Oregon
2009

CHILDHOOD

I was born on September 23, 1927 in Madison, Wisconsin. 1927 was a year with a few other events of note. It was the year that Lindbergh flew the ocean in a one seat airplane with no sleep, extremely minimal navigation equipment, and no communication gear. His flight was remarkable, and it was a sensation all through the 1927 year. This was also the year Stalin became dictator of Russia. Ford started making the model A and stopped the production of the model T. Model A's were then sold for $385. That year the New York, New Jersey Holland Tunnel was opened. The giant panda was discovered in China, and the night before I was born a world famous fight took place between Gene Tunney and Jack Dempsey, so the newspapers were full of headlines on the day of my birth discussing the fight of the night before. The first demonstration of a television was made in 1927 by Philo Farnsworth, but it was another 25 years before there was much commercial use of television. The Harlem Globetrotters played their first game in 1927. There was an 8.3 earthquake in China that killed over 200,000 people, and the first iron lung was installed in 1927. All these other events made more headlines than did my birth.

My folks were living in Madison, Wisconsin at the time. My father was a professor of chemistry at the University of Wisconsin. He had obtained his Ph.D. in physical chemistry at Harvard, then spent some time in World War I in the Army's Chemical Warfare Division. The gas mask he helped design was in use until well into World War

Dorin 1928

II before there were any major changes. Some old prototype gas masks were stored in our attic and would occasionally be found when we were rummaging around under the eaves: the big glassy eyes and long snout scared my sister. My mother had graduated Phi Beta Kappa from Oberlin College in Ohio. I had an older brother, and two older sisters. I was the last of four children, and because my mother had difficulty in previous pregnancies she had been

Daniels Children 1928

advised to not have another baby. It had even been suggested that she should have an abortion. Abortions were not legal, and my mother

1

having rather strict religious convictions, she would have nothing to do with that consideration, so I came along unimpeded.

My given name was a bit of a problem for me. The name Dorin was not a common name – in fact it was essentially unheard of. In trying to determine the origin of the name over many years several hypotheses were considered. One consideration was that my mother was under the influence of alcohol when she chose the name. That consideration seems very unlikely as she never to my knowledge ever took a drink, except one time when I was a teenager and went with her to a wedding of a family friend's son. She didn't dream that the punch might have alcohol in it. She liked the punch and kept going back for more until I realized that she shouldn't drive and took the keys to the car. I had a learner's permit for driving at the time. Several hours after we got home and her giddiness calmed down she got a funny look on her face and said "I think that punch had booooze in it …"

Another theory – namely that she was still under the influence of anesthesia when she chose my name - is very unlikely as the birth certificate says Boy Daniels which was later crossed through and Dorin inserted. Obviously the conclusion from that finding is that she had lots of time to figure a name. My oldest sister many years later said she recalled that my mother spent many days trying to come up with a name that sounded good with the last name Daniels, and the middle name of Slater which she wanted to use to honor her aunt and uncle with whom she lived during most of her childhood. I was very shy as a child and had difficulty trying to explain a name that no one knew. It was common to be told that Dorin couldn't be my name – it had to be Dorian, or Darwin or something else. When I went to high school I found that I had been assigned to the girls' gym class and my locker was in the girls' area. The school officials had assumed that I was a "Doris" or "Doreen." I was devastated. I also had a mild speech impediment and had trouble pronouncing the letter 'r' so not only couldn't I explain my name – I couldn't pronounce it either. I was studied by speech pathologists at the University, some of whom thought I must have lived in some small county in Kentucky because my speech was similar to a local dialect there. They used a brand new device to help me with my problem. It was a wire recorder – the predecessor to the tape recorder – so that I could hear myself as I sounded to others. Later, when I was delivering babies, I strongly recommend unambiguous and gender specific names for newborns.

2

The house I was brought home to, after the then mandatory 10 day hospital stay, was a colonial two story with a kitchen, dining room, living room and tiny lavatory on the first floor, and four bedrooms and one bathroom on the second floor. There was a basement which had a coal furnace, a coal bin (the coal came down a chute through a window), a small workshop, and a laundry area, plus space for a ping-pong table and a pantry which my brother modified later into a photographic darkroom. On the back porch there was a small door on both the inside and the outside of the wall that opened up so milk could be delivered. That receptacle could hold about four quarts of milk. Milk was delivered on a regular basis in glass bottles. There was

Madison House - 1944

an icebox in the kitchen which had a door on the outside for the 25 or 50 pounds of ice that were delivered on a regular basis. We enjoyed it when the iceman arrived because he would chip off some ice for us to chew. Ice was sawed from the frozen lakes in the winter and stored in sawdust to be delivered throughout the rest of the year. We never seemed to get sick on that ice which would now be considered "unsanitary." I don't know when we got a refrigerator but that was quite an improvement over the ice box. There was an attic which over the years was modified, and was used as sleeping quarters for my brother and myself. Much of the time in my childhood my paternal grandmother lived with us, and with two girls, two boys, parents and grandmother, the four-bedroom arrangement was inadequate. My brother had allergies, and the attic walls were made of a very cheap fiberboard, to which I'm sure he was highly allergic. Much of the time in the winter he and I slept outside on the screened in porch, even in subzero weather. We had feather comforters and other blankets so we nestled down and slept very comfortably in the freezing air. We sometimes used the porch in the summer as well, because the attic was quite hot, and there was no air conditioning in those days.

3

Our father was quite miserable in the summers due to a fairly severe ragweed allergy causing hay fever. In the early and mid 1930s there was really no effective medicine other than ephedrine to help his symptoms. Being a professor he had most of his summers off from his teaching schedule except when he taught the summer school program. He used his "free" summer time writing text books, researching, and supervising graduate students. During the worst of the hay fever season he found, as did many other hay fever victims, that by camping on the Door County peninsula in northern Wisconsin he could get some relief. Door County is surrounded by water with Green Bay on the west and Lake Michigan on the east, giving it an air conditioning effect. We camped for a few seasons in Peninsula State Park and while there one year we found a piece of beachfront wooded property two and a half miles north of Jacksonport on the Lake Michigan side of the peninsula which we were able to purchase. Over the next several summers we built the family cabin which we named D6 for the six Daniels.

The day after we arrived on the building site in 1935 my folks agreed to purchase new cedar logs which had been located in a swamp about a mile and a half from the lot. Those logs were cut and delivered by horse team a day or two later at a cost of seventy five cents each. (This was Depression time – gas was about twenty cents a gallon, post card stamps were one cent, and letter postage was three cents.) My mother had devised a basic floor plan and cabin size so stakes were set out and the whole family pitched in and cleared the forest floor with axes, hatchets, and shovels, down to underlying sand. We got some help from two local farmers who were also part time

D6 Cabin First Year - 1935

carpenters. My father and brother hauled sand and gravel from the beach, bought four sacks of cement, made a mixing platform, and poured concrete posts for the floor supports. The hired help got us started, teaching us how to notch the logs for good log cabin construction. They did most of the notching and placing of the logs, and helped us with the ridge pole and cut outs for doors and windows. They were only able to work part time because of their farm commitments and the total time they worked amounted to three and a half days labor each. All of us children were given jobs in the construction process. One of my jobs, along with my sisters, was to strip the bark off of the cedar logs. The bark was used to make the driveway a bit more serviceable - it was just a track through the woods. We used a draw knife and hatchets to smooth the rafter logs before putting on the roof lumber and asphalt shingle rolls. We were able to complete the entire process from ordering of the logs to completion of the roof within about two weeks, with only seven

Roofing Crew 1935 - Farrington Jr, F Sr, Dorin, Florence, Mino

man days of hired help.

We had also found an old pioneer cabin near Jacksonport which had degenerated into a pig pen, but it was basically intact in spite of a few rotten logs. We were able to disassemble the logs and had them brought to our property, storing them for the winter in the newly built "Loggery." The next year they were assembled into the kitchen wing we called the "Piggery." We lived in tents the first couple of years while building the cabin. Our beach was wonderful and we kids had a blast being in Door County most of the summers during much of our childhood.

The second year of cabin construction required more professional help with concrete porch, stone fireplace and chimney construction but a lot of the construction was still done by all of us. We didn't have inside water, plumbing or electricity for many years. We hauled water from a hand pump that we shared with the next door neighbor. We used a wood stove for cooking and heating. We had an outside privy – which was named The Pagoda because it seemed to stand out among the then-small trees; it did have a nice view of the woods. We used kerosene lamps for reading and evening activities.

During some of those early years my siblings and I would pick cherries in the busy part of the season. Door County was a very large cherry growing area in the 1930s. Children could work in those days, and no labor laws prevented us from climbing high ladders in order to do the cherry picking. I was not a good worker but I did do enough work to earn a dollar which I used to buy a dog from the orchard owner. The dog seemed to adopt our family and the owner didn't seem to like the dog. "Bucky" was the name we gave the dog because it cost

Deterpog

me a buck. He was a replacement for a wonderful cocker spaniel named Peter who was affectionately called "Deterpog" because of a 'balking tackwards' word game we used to play at the time. Peter had previously died of distemper. Bucky was in the family for a long time, and years later when all of us children had left town it was common for neighbor children to come to the house in Madison and ask my mother if Bucky could come out and play.

My brother, Farrington Jr., was nine years older than I was. My oldest sister Florence was seven years older and my other sister Miriam was three years older. They were all good students. I did not have the academic drive that my brother and sisters demonstrated, and the teachers that followed all of us through school were rather concerned that I was not as highly motivated a student as they had come to expect from my siblings. In fact the Daniels children were pretty much expected to be straight A students their entire academic careers, and I was too easily distracted and, well, let's face it, too lazy to be a straight A student.

Dorin and Bucky c 1940

The grade school that all of us went to was Nakoma Grade School, in a suburb of Madison which was quite far out in the country at the time. Our house was built in 1921. For a long time there were only a few houses on the block. Gradually the whole neighborhood filled in to a solid residential area. Our school was about a half-mile away and we walked or rode bicycles to and from and thought nothing of it. Wisconsin winters can be quite severe and it was not unusual to have two or three feet of snow on the ground and extremely cold temperatures. Usually when the temperature got colder than twenty degrees below zero the school was closed, with the intent that the children stay home and stay inside for protection. We always took that type of school closure as a holiday, and went out and played in the snow, skied, or skated, so twenty below to us was a holiday. If we had a cold spell without snow the lakes would freeze over and we had a wonderful skating rink several miles wide.

Farrington Jr. Florence Mino Dorin
Skating on Madison Lake

Our grade school went through eighth grade, and one of my activities was playing the violin which I started at age six. I was in the grade school orchestra, and in those days the string sections of the orchestras were quite well represented, much more than they seem to be nowadays where the musical curriculum is more likely to have a band emphasis. I continued to be in the first string violin section all through high school. I also sang in the chorus and was a member of the church choir for many years. My two sisters were both quite active in music; both played the piano quite well. My sister Miriam, the closest to me who went by the nickname of "Mino" was quite accomplished as a pianist and she carried this through her schooling as well.

Another fun musical instrument that I learned to play was the musical saw. In the mid 1930s my uncle J. Horton Daniels was visiting us in Madison and played his musical saw. I was fascinated and determined to learn to play it myself. My uncle got me started with his wonderful old carpenter's saw and after he left I just had to have one of my own. Uncle Horton was a medical missionary in China and had carried this saw with him for many years. Before his career was over he had survived two Japanese invasions of China and several years in captivity in the Philippines where he was caught trying to get home when WWII started. The entertainment that he provided with that saw probably had something to do with his relatively good treatment in captivity. He was able to keep his saw through all of his trials and tribulations. After he left, my mother took me on a hunt of the hardware stores and we walked all over downtown Madison looking for a suitable saw. As we walked from one hardware store to the next it was sort of like a pied piper scenario with my mother leading, me following and carrying a violin bow, and both of us being followed by an ever increasing crowd who were following us from store to store to watch and listen as this little kid tried to make music with any fairly flexible saw available. We never did find a suitable saw at the hardware stores and finally bought one which was made as a musical saw. It was not nearly as good as the carpenter's saw my uncle had carried with him for years. I still play that saw occasionally as a novelty.

Playing the Saw

My mother had lots of interests other than raising kids and housework. In Depression days domestic help was easy to obtain and quite inexpensive. Dad had a salaried job and even though it was not a great amount of money we were better off than a lot of other people who were struggling. Dad was always concerned about the less fortunate so the hiring of domestic help had dual purpose - to give Mother some relief with the household duties but also to help someone else who desperately needed a job. For many years we had "Linnie" who was brought to the house by her husband in time to help get us kids some breakfast and get us ready for school. She would do the routine housework and prepare meals. She would get the food for supper prepared and then leave before we sat down to eat. For many years she was almost part of the family and was a great help for my mother.

8

My recollections as a young child are of playing outside much of the year. We had an empty lot right next to our house. It was one of the last lots in our neighborhood to be filled with a house, and actually was not filled until long after I left Madison. This field became a magnet for neighborhood children to play baseball and other activities such as mumblety-peg (a game with many variations where pocket knives were thrown to stick in the ground), and fox & geese in the snow. Occasionally it became a crude ice skating rink. All school boys carried pocket knives year around. They were just part of the dress, and were used to play games, practice throwing skills for sticking into the ground or trees, for whittling, carving initials into trees, and making marshmallow sticks. Try sending a boy to school now with a pocket knife and the kid gets kicked out of school and you and the boy are labeled criminals. We never considered doing any harm with these wonderful devices. If your parents were able to buy "official" Boy Scout gear you could get knee high leather Boy Scout boots complete with a knife sheath built into the top of the boot and it contained an official Boy Scout knife. This made you the envy of the neighborhood but even though you could do all sorts of survival things with the scout knife, they were too heavy and poorly balanced to be good throwing knives. Speaking of boots and shoes, they were made of leather and most didn't have much lining and usually didn't have much of an arch support. The soles were made of some sort of composition material that usually wore out before the upper part of the shoe was worn out. Most shoes had two or three sole replacements before the shoe was discarded or passed down to the next kid. You knew it was time to get new soles when you wore a hole in the bottom of the shoe and the socks showed through. When my dad needed new shoes he would usually buy the first pair brought to him by the shoe salesman. He was so unwilling to cause anyone any inconvenience that he seldom asked a clerk to show him something else. Even at a young age I thought that his unwillingness to inconvenience anyone else was probably a bit unusual.

When I was in first grade Maurice Farrar moved into our block and he became my childhood chum. He was one day older than I was. Maurice had moved from Wyoming and for several years he and I were planning to leave school early and become cowboys in Wyoming. Our block was irregularly shaped and our houses were not far apart when we used shortcuts through other people's property. We spent many hours together, in and out of both houses. His father was an entomologist, specializing in bee keeping. His mother was a great cook and it was always a pleasure to be in their house. Maurice had a basketball hoop in his driveway and we spent many hours shooting baskets. We actually became pretty good. Neither one of us did much in the way of school athletics. I did go out for basketball my first year in high school but I was way too short, and not aggressive enough to be good at competitive sports.

I can recall that on very cold and absolutely clear nights, without the air and light pollution that we have nowadays, Maurice and I would lie down in the field next to my house and look at the stars for hours. The sky was so filled with stars that it's almost impossible to imagine how many more stars we could see then, compared to what we can usually see now. We were quite good at identifying the major constellations, and during these observations, at a very early age, we tried to contemplate, and struggled to understand, the meaning of space, infinity, distance, light years, etc. I have fond memories of those early days, and when I look back on those cold nights I wonder why our parents didn't object to our lying out in subzero weather, in the snow, with the potential of freezing to death. We were always reasonably comfortable, even though in those days we had leather boots without linings and we had some wool clothing, but none of the modern fabrics that we have nowadays, so that cold and wet were not as well handled as they are now.

Maurice and Dorin Mid 30s

In the summer, especially during warbler migration season, we would ride our bikes the few miles to the University of Wisconsin Arboretum where we would count the number of bird species we could identify. There were also Indian mounds, trails, and cold springs with watercress in the Arboretum. Maurice went to a different high school than I did, and we both went into the service during the war and lost track of each other for several years. We met again briefly when I was working at Oak Ridge, Tennessee and he was taking a residency in Obstetrics in Atlanta after finishing medical school. He established a busy practice in Phoenix and I was able to see him on several occasions over many years when I attended meetings in Phoenix. He and his wife Connie were very gracious hosts whenever I could visit them. I was quite saddened by his recent death.

We had a crabapple tree in our back yard. I think kids have a primordial instinct to climb trees and our crabapple tree was a good climber. I recall several occasions when someone would come and spray some awful smelling stuff on the tree and we were told to stay away for some period of time. Some years the tree was heavily loaded with apples and one year I thought I would make my fortune by picking a lot of them and selling them at the local store. I picked what I thought to be a lot of apples and arranged with the store to have them sold. A few days later the store owner came to the house and gave me a very firm but gentle lecture about produce quality. My apples were full of worms and were not saleable. We had other apple trees too – a Northern Spy by the little pool and a Duchess at the corner of the lot where the driveway meets Waban Hill.

Everyone in my family was small. Both my folks were the shortest in their families. My folks were concerned that I would be too short – there was only one boy in my class shorter than I was all through grade school. A family friend, Dr. Elmer Severinghaus, was an endocrinologist at the University and he was doing experiments on human growth hormone. He enrolled me into his research group with the hope that I would gain a few inches over my expected height. For many months I went to his lab on a regular basis to be measured and weighed and to get some painful shots. My fingertip to fingertip (wingspan) measurements were as important to the researchers as was my actual height. I guess they didn't want me to grow long arms and look like an ape. After several months of this painful ritual I became a bit emotionally unsettled and the experiment was stopped. The shots probably did have some effect as I grew to five foot seven and a half inches, making me easily the tallest in the family. I can't figure out how those shots got to the next generation – my son Alan and his three boys are all well over six feet tall.

There was an older boy who lived on the other side of the vacant lot next to our house. He was several years older than my brother and he had a motorcycle. Looking back I suspect that it was a late 1920s Indian motorcycle. It was his pride and joy and he was frequently gone for long periods of time. When he was home the motorcycle was usually in pieces and being fixed for some problem. My only other early exposure to motorcycles was that there was a dirt motorcycle race track with sharp curves and hills and bumps not very far from my house. I guess there were fairly regular races but I only remember getting to those races once. I suspect they cost more money to attend than most of us could spare in the Depression. What I do remember that impressed me was that there were nurses there to take care of injuries. These nurses were in crisp starched white dress uniforms (that was usual for the day). As I watched the races it was easy to see that those starched white uniforms were getting less white each time the motorcycles went past the nurses spewing thick dust. I also recall, with more detail than I would expect these many years later, that when a rider bounced off the track and sort of wound up in a ball a few feet off the track the nurses ran to help them and guess what – the first thing they did to this moaning piece of humanity was to stick a glass thermometer into his mouth and take his pulse. My medical training at that time probably consisted of an introduction to Cub Scout first aid but it seemed intuitively then (and still does) that the first thing to do in that situation would be to check to be sure that all extremities, including the head, are pointed in the right direction and that no new joints had suddenly been created. Then look for spurting red stuff and then check for pulse and breathing. If they are moaning you know they are breathing. To stick a glass mercury thermometer into the mouth of a semiconscious person didn't seem to warrant first priority. In those days a broken thermometer wasn't considered a hazmat catastrophe (we liked to play with the mercury), but it still wasn't smart to chew up thermometers. Years later when I got training in the Navy Hospital Corps I had a bit more understanding of the nurse's behavior. Most nurse type training starts on hospitalized patients and the first part of the assessment is TPR (temperature, pulse, and respiration.) TPR, TPR, TPR is drummed into the early training but it still didn't seem to fit the motorcycle situation.

Neither of my parents drank any alcohol nor were they interested in cocktail parties. They were not concerned much with social circles but as my father's status in scientific organizations kept rising they were exposed more and more to social events, including White House dinners. In an attempt to get me exposed to proper etiquette I was enrolled in an extracurricular club that taught social graces and basic dance steps. I suppose that this was probably about 7th or 8th grade. My sister Mino apparently was put through the same ordeal ahead of me. I do recall that we would meet in the evening perhaps every month or two. I was very shy and it was very stressful for me to ask a girl to dance. I had one very embarrassing situation that still bothers me when I think about it. We were being instructed on how to behave while introducing a partner in a reception line. Before I got to the end of the line I became aware of giggles, twittering, and laughter and suddenly realized that I had been introducing my partner to everyone in the receiving line with "may I produce Miss So and So." I think that may have been the night that someone snuck in some hard cider so the giggles may not have all been at my expense. I think that if I were to be graded on that class I would get an A in wallflower, A in blushing and B in dance (I really had pretty good coordination).

When we finished Nakoma Grade School, after eighth grade, we had the choice of two high schools. One was West High School which was about three miles away and the other was Wisconsin High School, about five miles away, which was affiliated with the University of Wisconsin, and was actually a practice teaching laboratory for the Department of Education at the University. All of our family went to Wisconsin High School because of our university affiliation, and because it was a good academic institution. Again, most of the teachers who taught my brother and sisters were quite concerned that I was not following in their footsteps as a straight A student. In 1941 when World War II broke out I was still in early high school. The demeanor of almost everything in the country was changed. The war effort took precedence over most everything else. We had gas, sugar and meat rationing. There were no new cars available, tires were almost impossible to find, and everything went to the war effort. Our family had always used public transportation to and from town, and to and from the high school, so there was not any major interruption of our style of living. There was a bus stop about two blocks from our house so we didn't have far to walk for public transportation. We only had one car in the family, and as my brother and oldest sister became drivers, making four drivers with one car, it made public transportation an increased necessity. As children we used the bus to go all over town, for various reasons such as school, music lessons, to movies or recreational events all by the age of nine or ten. I think I even took the bus alone to violin lessons in downtown Madison as early as age eight. My father frequently took the bus to and from work so that Mother could have the car to do errands and shuffle kids. My mother was not a good driver. My oldest sister thinks she only had a one day training session. Fortunately she didn't have any serious accidents. Before my

13

high school was completed I had a driver's license, which now made six drivers with one car. This did not create as great a problem as it might seem, because in the latter part of the war years my brother was a doctor in the Army Medical service, my oldest sister was working in Washington, D.C., and my other sister was away at college.

When I was quite young I remember that my father was always working. Today he would be classified as a workaholic. He often said that taking the time to eat was a waste of time and if possible he would rather take a pill and keep on working. He still managed to find time to play with us kids before bedtime. He became expert at letting us escape while we were trying to run past him while he was lying down on the living room floor. He would often then take us up to bed and read us a story. After putting us to bed he would retire to his study and work on the textbooks he was writing or revising. He had an extremely strict code of ethics – he never worked on his textbooks while at work at the university and he never took royalties from patents that resulted from work that he or his graduate students did at the university. Years after he died a nephew of mine did some research and learned that the patents that my father had turned over to the university amounted to an incredible figure which was thought to be in excess of a billion dollars. In some of my weaker moments I catch myself wishing that maybe he could have kept just a little bit of that patent money. I know that many professors kept a lot of the patent money that resulted from their research.

Even though my father was always working and serious he managed to have some fun and had a twinkle in his eye. If we were on a car trip any situation, such as the odometer turning to an even hundred miles, could trigger a stop at the nearest ice cream parlor for a celebration. He loved ice cream and loved to have an excuse to treat us. He maintained that ice cream had no calories because it was cold. He was always optimistic – every rainstorm was "just a little clearing up shower." If an experiment didn't turn out as expected he was never discouraged – he took it as a challenge to investigate in a new direction. He often lamented the fact that research money usually came with specific outcome requirements rather than for "pure science" that he loved so much. "Pure science" allowed the researcher to chase a result of an experiment in whatever direction it wanted to go.

Dad would not even think of doing anything that would hurt anyone but as I said – he had a twinkle in his eyes and one Halloween he helped me set up a harmless prank. He prepared two concoctions in some sort of a jelly and when the gels were mixed together in a paper towel it created a very unpleasant rotten egg type smell (hydrogen sulfide I think). Some friends and I took that stuff and went around the neighborhood mixing small amounts of each component in paper towels and throwing it into people's garages. He would never have allowed us to do anything that was actually destructive. Another harmless prank that was common in those days was to make notches in an old empty wooden thread spool. Then when you put a nail into the hole and you wound string around the spool and held the spool to someone's window – wow! did that ever make a loud noise in the house when you pulled the string. You had better be able to run fast because it was almost a given that someone would explode out of the door of the house within seconds after you rattled their windows. In those days no one sued if a homeowner caught you and paddled your behind.

My mother was not as likely to spend much time with us in the evenings as she frequently was tired or not feeling well. In spite of her chronic fatigue she was very creative. She braided rugs; she painted murals on our dining room walls, on the chapel wall at the First Congregational Church, and on the walls of a library in another town. She did creative family Christmas cards every year for many years. She spent lots of time researching the family genealogy and wrote quite a few books on the genealogy of both sides of the family. Later she wrote up the travels she took with my dad on his lecture tour travels. She also did water color and oil painting and made an excellent bronze bust of my dad for the chemistry department at the University of Wisconsin when they dedicated the new chemistry building with his name.

Farrington Daniels Chemistry Building

I think it is fair to say that most people judge their childhood at the time they are growing up as being normal. I always thought my childhood was normal, but as I grew older and saw what other people experienced, compared to what I experienced, I now have to admit that my childhood was unusually blessed. For example it was not unusual for us to come home from school and find a visiting professor from another country joining us for supper and it was quite common to have professors from other American universities visiting. We were never discouraged from entering into conversation with these visitors.

My father belonged to a dinner club whose members were professors in the arts and humanities as well as various sciences. They rotated from one member's house to another so on occasion the group would be at our house. To me that was normal, but to have that much intellectual horsepower in one's house was certainly not what most people would consider normal. I recall several times when I would sneak down the stairs so I could listen to the discussion. I was usually caught and sent back upstairs to bed. Both my parents had been brought up in quite strict religious atmospheres. We were coming out of the Victorian era and there was still some Victorian type influence. One major difference that I can see in retrospect was that in the Victorian era children were to be seen but not heard at the dinner table. This was not the rule in our house. Dinner was fairly formal, everybody sat down, and everybody dressed up. We were encouraged to express our views and enter into the conversation. This early life intellectual interchange was very helpful in learning to converse, and to bring out intellectual curiosity. For this our parents were a very positive influence. Another positive influence from them was insistence of total honesty. We were not threatened – it was just assumed that there was no choice other than total honesty.

I did a little bit of dating in high school but I suspect that I wasn't much fun for the girls because of my shyness. I would like to discuss scientific subjects and most of the girls wanted to go to movies or to dances. Movies were a main source of entertainment and in the 1930s and early 1940s there were some excellent shows. War movies had the expected violence but most other movies had some nice plots and the good guys always won. I really did like the musical movies and wish that that type of movie would make a comeback and replace some of the violence and trash coming from current Hollywood. I thought I was pretty good at chess but one evening I went to pick up a date and the girl was a bit slow on the primping that girls do so I visited with her older brother while waiting for her to come downstairs. We figured we could start a chess game because he thought she would be pretty

16

slow so we set up the board and started a game. I thought we could finish the game in 15 or 20 minutes but I was really humiliated when he beat me in something like four moves. Really experienced chess players are all aware of these moves and avoid getting caught.

One of my good high school friends was "Buzz" Baldwin. His father was a professor in bacteriology at the University. Buzz raised pigeons as a hobby. He became sick sometime late in grade school and was diagnosed as having tuberculosis so he was put to bed for over a year. To overcome boredom he read the Encyclopedia Britannica from cover to cover several times. He was very bright and retained an incredible amount of the knowledge from the Britannica. Today he would be considered a "brainiac" but I don't think that term was in use at the time. He became physically soft from inactivity but did very

well scholastically. Near the end of the war the army decided that he was physically fit and he was drafted, only to do essentially nothing, leaving him bored and frustrated. He went on to become a Rhodes Scholar and a college professor. We corresponded for a brief time at the end of the war while we were both still in

Buzz Baldwin and Friend at Jacksonport Wisconsin c 1943

the service but I lost track of him for 50 or so years till we got in touch about our mutual friend Maurice Farrar's illness. He told me that he was in good health and did a lot of hiking in the mountains.

It is sort of interesting as I try to remember what I did in my childhood to realize how totally blank I am for some periods of time and how ridiculous some of the memories actually are. When I was about seven years old my dad taught for a semester at Cornell University in Ithaca, New York. I know that the family spent weekends exploring New England and took a trip to Washington D.C. but about the only thing I remember from that period of time was that the house we stayed in had a nice dining room and there was a bump in the floor under the carpet near the chair where the lady of the house sat. If we pushed on the bump a buzzer rang in the kitchen. It was a call system for the lady of the house to call the maid from the kitchen. Why I remembered that and nothing of much significance I don't really understand.

Horses – I loved horses. Maybe it was because of my early conviction that I was going to move to Wyoming and become a cowboy. We would occasionally go to a riding stable near the cabin in Door County

Door County Riding Stable - FD Jr,Florence,Mino,Dorin

and I thought I was getting pretty good at handling horses. There was a riding stable in Madison that I went to for awhile. I would ride the public bus and transfer to another branch line to get to the stable. It was a great deal for the stable owners when I showed up at their large closed arena in the winter to ride – they got paid to have me exercise their horses for them. I did learn how to ride some multi-gaited horses and it was quite satisfying to control some of those wonderful animals. When I was in about 7th grade we went to Minneapolis to visit some relatives. I had a cousin who was fairly close to my age and his dad ran a nursery. They had some big draft horses (about the size of the big horses you see in the beer commercials) and my cousin Franc and I decided to ride them. They were work horses and I don't think they had been ridden. I was a bit cocky about my abilities so somehow we managed to get up on them and started to ride bareback. The horses didn't like the idea and started galloping and managed to throw us off. Not only was my pride wounded – I broke a rib and had a miserable long ride home from Minneapolis to Madison – a distance of almost 300 miles.

While I was in high school, as the war was progressing, the first year or two were quite discouraging while our country was building up our military forces, and suffering losses in the Pacific that were horrendous. At the same time we were preparing for the invasion of Europe. In the early part of the war we were also suffering much in the way of shipping losses. The Nazi submarines were sinking large numbers of our cargo ships along our eastern seaboard and in the Atlantic Ocean shipping lanes. One of the research projects that my dad and some of his graduate students were working on was a project to devise a method for detecting submarines. The theory being tested was that all ships including submarines would leave a trace amount of oil in their path whether they were on the surface or submerged, This oil had some fluorescent tendencies so my dad was trying to develop a skimmer that would sample the surface water from a boat pulling the device, run it through a collector and shine an ultraviolet light on the sample and chart the results. I was underage but somehow my dad got me approved to run the University motorboat while he and his students fiddled with the equipment. It was "tough duty" to run that university speed boat all over Lake Mendota trying to find other boat tracks. My dad also did this while at our Cabin, going out on Lake Michigan to the bemusement of the Jacksonport fisherman whose boat he hired. The experiment did not prove to be practical but it was a nice try and I had been able to contribute something to the war effort.

The war news we would get from newspapers was usually several days old, and news reels at the movie theater were usually about a week or two old. We had some radio broadcasts but there was no television at that time, or computers, or Internet, and the long-distance phone was expensive and not used very much. Many high school students would enter the armed services before graduation, sometimes being awarded their diplomas later, and sometimes posthumously. The toll on the male population was severe. As the war progressed I became a little more serious about what I was going to do with my life and decided that I would graduate early, taking some summer school classes and some heavier loads, and I actually buckled down and became a reasonably good student. I graduated from high school in three years.

Towards the end of my high school years my father was called to Chicago to become the Director of the Metallurgical Lab - part of the Manhattan Project at the University of Chicago. This was located at Stagg field where the first chain reaction had already taken place. He was very active and high up in the Manhattan Project, and on a first name basis with many of the intellectual heavyweights like Fermi, Compton, Urey, and Oppenheimer. When my father was at Chicago he would occasionally come home to visit and occasionally my mother would go to Chicago to visit him

My mother stayed in Madison for the summer after my early high school graduation, while I went to the University of Wisconsin for the summer semester. That was a rather strange experience because there were almost no men on campus except those who were already in the service and attending a training program at the university. Almost all of the able-bodied males were in the armed services, and I was under age so I was one of the very few civilian males on campus that summer. I was very shy and I didn't really know how to capitalize on

19

that male/female ratio. In the fall of 1944 my mother moved to Chicago, and I went with her because I was a little bit burned out on school. Mother rented our Madison house and moved to Chicago to be with Dad 'for the duration.' My folks had an apartment not far from the University of Chicago campus. During the time that I was in Chicago, in the fall of 1944, I went to a secretarial school to learn how to type. Typing was the only course I took as I was not interested in shorthand or other business courses. Again there were only girls in the class. I had not taken typing in high school and I felt that it would be important for later use.

Also in the fall of 1944 I took a trip to visit my brother who was taking his internship at the New York Hospital which was affiliated with Cornell Medical School. He had been taken into the army part way through his medical school training and finished medical school at Harvard. When I visited him he was extremely busy so I was pretty much on my own and went to several Broadway shows including *Oklahoma*. Concerning that trip I don't recall a lot of detail but I do remember that I got a very bad case of bronchitis, or flu, or pneumonia and spent several days in my brother's apartment trying to recover. We had some sulfa drugs by then but no other antibiotics were available so my brother treated me with old fashioned whiskey. That was quite an experience coming from a teetotaling family, being underage and being told to "drink up kid, it may not cure you but you might feel better." I took a few other trips during the war before I was old enough for service myself. I visited my sister Florence in Washington, D.C. and visited the Senate Chambers and several of the museums. I even got a tour of the new Pentagon where a distant uncle was stationed. I doubt a teenager would be allowed in the Pentagon now even if his uncle was a general. Florence and her husband Jim took me to a Washington Senators baseball game and I, being pretty ignorant of baseball strategies, couldn't understand why the crowd was going nuts when to me nothing was happening. The pitcher was in the process of winning a "no hitter" game and I wanted to see some hits. All of those trips I made were by railroad, alone, and on coaches.

When I turned 17 that fall I was old enough to get into the Navy with parental consent. I took the test for what was called radio technician. By passing a fairly difficult test, called the Eddy test, with quite good scores, I was soon allowed into the Navy with a Seaman First-Class rating, which was a couple of steps up from the usual entry level.

1928

F.Jr, Mino, Dorin, Florence - 1929

1930

1934

Dad & Dorin Early 1930s

Dorin in Scout Uniform

Mid 1930s

High School Graduation - 1944

Daniels Family 1943 - Dorin, Florence, Mino, Dad, Mother, Farrington Jr.

Farrington jr.   Florence
Dorin and Miriam
Daniels
Wish you oceans of happiness
in
1931.

Christmas joy and goodwill
from the Daniels on Waban Hill
1937

Greetings from the Daniels — 1938

1941

Greetings from the Daniels

Daniels Family Christmas Cards
From My Childhood

22

NAVY

When I entered the Navy in January of 1945, WWII was still going full swing with no good estimate of when it might be over. I was sent to the Great Lakes Naval Training Station, north of Chicago on Lake Michigan, first for basic training, and then for radar electronics training. The term radar was not being used as it was still considered secret, and trainees were called radio technicians rather than radar

Matchbook Cover - Navy Training School

technicians. In essence this was a very fast-paced electrical engineering course, and as there were no calculators or computers, all calculations were done by slide rule and by hand. Part of the time that I was in the radio technician training program I was assigned to Wright Junior College in Chicago and was able to visit my folks on occasion. Mathematics was not my forte and it became apparent within the first month or two that electrical engineering was not where I should be, so the Navy assigned me to the Hospital Corps which was a much better fit for my interests and capabilities. They did not take away my advanced rating (Seaman First Class, which was two steps above entry) when they switched me to the Hospital Corps so I had a jump start on advancement. Before I was actually transferred to San Diego for my Hospital Corps training I was able to get a bit of recreation time and saw some stage shows including *Othello* with Paul Robeson, Jose Ferrer and Uta Hagen, all well known performers of the era. Uta Hagen was born in

I Watched This Show In Chicago

Germany but raised in Madison, Wisconsin and was a classmate and friend of my brother.

I did well at the San Diego Hospital Corps School and was later transferred to the naval hospital at Newport, Rhode Island. While in San Diego I lived in a huge building in Balboa Park that had bunks for more than a thousand sailors. We slept in triple-decker bunk beds and were awakened every morning by loud blaring loudspeakers playing the song "The Atchison Topeka and the Santa Fe." The whole park had been taken over by the Navy for training facilities. Our building

was close to the Ford Bowl, since named the Starlight Bowl, a band shell that I presume still stands.

During my initial training at Great Lakes, the war in Europe ended and the date that occurred – May 7/8,

Ford Bowl - Balboa Park - 1945 - Sailors Sunbathing

1945 - was called VE Day, for Victory in Europe. The war emphasis was then concentrated on the Far East where we were anticipating extremely difficult times and extremely heavy losses if we actually invaded Japan. While I was in Hospital Corps training in San Diego the atomic bombs were dropped on Hiroshima and Nagasaki, and not long after that the Japanese surrendered. We then had VJ Day – August 14, 1945 which was "Victory in Japan" day. San Diego erupted with emotions that had been bottled up for years. I was in downtown San Diego on VJ evening and saw some jubilant servicemen tip over a few cars, and saw girls disappear into crowds of servicemen, eventually coming out the other side of the crowd somewhat disheveled and with their lipstick smeared and their dresses ruffled but everyone seemed happy. There was some damage done but the emotions were so high that the military took it in stride, and the damage to the public facilities was not great. The celebration was incredible all over the country. My father, who was high up in the Manhattan Project, knew when the bombs were going to go off and he was called upon for news interviews once the world knew of this new weapon. He and many other scientists had strong concerns about the long term implications once the atomic secret was out. It was well understood by the scientists that other countries with less benevolent motives would clamor to acquire the capability to make atomic weapons. In one of his first news interviews he made an oft-quoted prophetic comment when asked about the long term implications of the bomb. His response was that he thought we had saved many of our sons but he was not so sure about the grandsons. It is pretty much agreed that had we not ended the war dramatically with the atomic bombs, somewhat over a million more American lives would have been lost in the attempt to invade Japan.

When I finished my hospital corps training in San Diego I was transferred to the Naval Hospital in Newport, Rhode Island. The trips between bases were interesting ordeals. Most troop movements were done by train. (There were very few transports done by airplane in those days.) The servicemen were usually put in old passenger cars that had been brought out of retirement. We referred to them as cattle cars because we were packed in tightly and really had no place to lie down, and our trips across country took many days. We were fed box lunches. We would occasionally stop and wait for other trains to pass which gave us a chance to get out and walk around a bit which really felt good after being cramped up for many hours. My recollection was that my pay was something like thirty-six dollars a month, and this was considerably more than the usual starting pay. On the cross country trips I had my first exposure to gambling. I was amazed and shocked at the amount of money that appeared from the pockets of these "poor" servicemen. There would be groups of six or so down on the floor in the aisle with lots of large bills. They were flipping cards or rolling dice and large sums of money would pass from one person to another. I had never seen that much money in one place before, and I didn't know how to play the games they were playing, so I never tried to enter into the activity. I was afraid – probably with good justification – that I would lose my shirt if I tried to play.

Within a relatively few months at Newport I become a Pharmacist's

Newport Naval Hospital Complex c. 1946

Mate Third Class, which was really quite an accomplishment, having been in the Navy less than a year and a half. I had seen a notice on the bulletin board that there was going to be an examination for Pharmacist's Mate Third Class in a few days so I did some quick studying and took the exam without much actual preparation and passed with a good score. When I received the promotion I worked as a night Master at Arms at the hospital, and was given far more responsibility than would have been expected for a youngster of my age and experience. The picture of me with my Master at Arms badge shows the *USS Constellation* in the background across the bay from the hospital complex.

I worked with doctors of incredible capability, many whom had wartime experiences that were hard to fathom. We had patients from the war on our wards that were pretty seriously injured, or with terminal illnesses, including lung abscess and other serious infections, and other complications of wartime injuries. Our hospital had a small supply of the new "wonder drug" called penicillin and I gave some patients rather painful shots of this new drug every two or four hours. When I came off of night duty I was assigned to an interesting job of driving doctors to and from the city hospital where they took care of families of servicemen. I had my first exposure to obstetrical care and obstetrical emergency complications while helping these doctors. In some cases I scrubbed in with the doctors as they performed surgery. Some of the doctors were very young having gone through accelerated wartime training programs. These young doctors were officers but most had no real interest in military protocol so they often clashed with the full time military senior medical officers. Some of the young doctors were rather mischievous and would sneak up on nurses in the middle of the night and spray them with ethyl chloride spray which was a cold freezing anesthetic. The nurses were startled and screamed appropriately but they couldn't do much as they were junior to the doctors. Several of the doctors spent a lot of time with me discussing patient's problems, medical diagnosis and treatment, and encouraging me to go into the field of medicine.

On a few occasions while at Newport I hitch hiked to New York with a few friends and attended some Broadway shows. In those days servicemen were treated well by the traveling public and it was quite easy to get rides. I do not recommend hitch hiking today. I was also able to get a chance to do some sight seeing in Newport. One time a few of us were able to hike on the famous Cliff Walk. I had been

Master at Arms - USS Constellation Across Bay

working extremely long hours before that hike so I was tired but still enjoyed the venture.

Newport Cliff Walk - 1946

One of the after-hours activities I was involved with at Newport was with a group of hospital corpsmen that would meet on occasion in the evening in a classroom and have a hypnosis session. There was one fellow who had a natural talent for hypnotizing people. His skills were great and he could hypnotize most people quickly. These sessions were great fun but left me somewhat uneasy and I was not quite sure at the time exactly why I was uncomfortable. The sessions were of the stage hypnotist variety where he would make people cackle like a chicken, or get very hot in a cold room, or demonstrate some extreme amount of strength on command. What intuitively bothered me then was a situation in which he demonstrated the extreme power of post hypnotic suggestion. Under hypnosis he had instructed the subject that when he woke up, he would be sitting and the hypnotist would be standing. From then on whenever the hypnotist would sit down the subject was to stand up. When the subject was awakened he was unaware of any instructions that he had been given, but whenever the hypnotist sat down the subject would immediately stand up. The subject seemed embarrassed and didn't know why he felt compelled to stand up. When we all tried to leave the room together, I began to realize that there could be some unintended consequences when a person without adequate training might create problems with hypnosis. The subject absolutely would not stand up to leave while the hypnotist was standing. The hypnotist had not put a time factor on the orders, nor had he arranged for some mechanism to reverse the command after the patient was awake. The subject had to be re-hypnotized to be able to leave the room with the group. I resisted being hypnotized myself even years later when I took a course in hypnosis from our very fine hospital chaplain in Ontario, Oregon where I practiced medicine for many years. Father Kirk had an advanced degree in psychology and was qualified to give instruction. I also never felt comfortable trying to hypnotize anyone else, even after I was trained to do so, but I did research the field in some depth and referred several patients for appropriate hypnotherapy. As I studied hypnosis more I came to realize how strong the post hypnotic suggestion can be, and what devastating effects it can have on people that aren't even formally or knowingly hypnotized. Under stressful circumstances people are often very vulnerable to suggestions that carry long term consequences. An example might be a young boy who is with a dying father and while under extreme emotional stress is given orders from the father to "always take care of your mother!" The boy grows up but never leaves home, never marries, and does not understand the compulsion he has to care for his mother. Such suggestions can be very powerful and disruptive and are frequently not understood by practitioners who are trying to help a distressed individual.

I was discharged from the Navy in July of 1946, having entered the service in January 1945. I had led a sheltered life so transitioning into the service was a bit of a shock, but the experience was a great "growing up" lesson and I actually recommend some service time for almost everyone. While in the Navy I had a few experiences that were eye openers. I had lived a clean life and had not been exposed to the rougher things in life so I was very surprised when returning to Great Lakes after my Boot Camp leave that I was treated rather gruffly, even like a criminal when I presented my papers at the gate. When the guard looked at my papers he suddenly got less pleasant and accused me of having been AWOL. I had been hospitalized in the University of Wisconsin Infirmary with viral pneumonia while on leave. The University had military training programs on campus and had contracted for medical care for serviceman but they were not very military oriented and somehow neglected to do the proper paper work indicating that I was under their medical care and really wasn't AWOL. I had never been accused of criminal activity before and it was an experience I didn't want to repeat.

While working in the Newport Naval Hospital, on one of the few days we had off, a friend and I walked along the roads where some of the fabulous mansions were located and were enjoying just looking. More like castles, these huge mansions were extremely elegant. Not surprisingly they were all surrounded by fences. Being overwhelmed with awe we sort of crowded into the bushes and up to the fences to get a better look. Our only intent was to get a better look but the local police picked us up on suspicion of malicious intent. Again I was in an uncomfortable situation. After much questioning, including some not-so-veiled threats, the police let us go without any charges but I had never undergone questioning by the police before and didn't enjoy the experience.

At the hospital in Newport there was a young doctor, Dr. Tenney, whose father was a well-known pediatrician in Madison, my home town, and he thought he was going to be discharged before I was. When he found that his discharge was going to be delayed and that he was going to be transferred to another location, he asked me if I would return his car to Madison for him. His car, a Packard coupe, had a large motor and small trunk. The driver sat well back of the center of the car and the hood of the car was very long to cover the big engine. After I was discharged from the Boston processing center I returned to Newport to pick up his car and started my trip westward. I do not recall a lot of detail from that trip but I do vividly recall that the car stalled on the George Washington Bridge in New York City. The guards were just about to have me hauled off at considerable expense when rather magically the car finally started and I was able to proceed to Princeton, New Jersey to spend the night with my sister Florence and her husband Jim. I don't recall much more about the route that I

took home except that I stopped at Oberlin, Ohio to visit my sister Miriam who was in summer school and finishing her senior year at Oberlin College. I had already submitted application papers for Oberlin but didn't know if I would be accepted. I do recall that my sister introduced me to some very attractive young ladies and I began to realize that going to college might well have some fringe benefits. My parents were still in Chicago at the time, but they were

Oberlin "Recruiters" - Mino At My Left

getting ready to move back to Wisconsin as the War was over and the Met Lab was phasing out. The Madison house had been rented out while my folks were in Chicago so I stopped in Chicago and then drove up to the Door County cabin were I stayed for a few weeks before returning to Madison to deliver the Tenney car to its home. I received notice that I had been accepted at Oberlin College so I was about to start my next phase of life – college away from home. I had been in the greatest naval force the world had ever seen. I had gone from coast to coast on my military assignments. It seems a bit ironic that my only time spent on a ship of any kind was on the Jamestown Ferry near Newport and the Coronado Ferry near San Diego.

Portrait c.1945

COLLEGE YEARS

I chose Oberlin College after the war because it was a smaller school

Oberlin Gym - Temporary Quarters

than the University of Wisconsin, and several family members had attended and were very happy with the school. My mother had attended and graduated Phi Beta Kappa in 1913. My sister was graduating about the same time that I was getting out of the Navy. There had been various cousins, aunts, and assorted relatives that had also graduated from Oberlin and a second cousin and his wife (Bob and Lucy Leonard) were on campus when I started. When I arrived the school was inundated with an overabundance of incoming students. Colleges all over the country were being hit with the same problem as thousands of returning servicemen were trying to catch up on their lives after many years serving their country in WWII. The creation of the GI Bill also brought many persons to colleges who would not previously have had the opportunity to get a higher education. The college improvised to provide the extra housing needed and I found myself in a converted gymnasium with bunks and foot lockers. It was almost a return to my large military quarters at San Diego but on a smaller scale. Construction had already started on new dormitories that we moved into later. We were assigned eating locations – meals at

Friend Moving From Gym to Dorm

Oberlin were fairly formal, sit down style, with proper dress requirements. Many students partially worked their way through school "working tables." The classes were of manageable size and taught by excellent faculty. The most impressive thing I observed at Oberlin was the quality of the students. A very high percentage of the students would have to be classified as outstanding individuals. Many of the entering class were older than the usual college freshmen because they had been in the service for several years and had grown up far too fast and had a high level of maturity and purpose.

New Dorm - Almost Ready for Occupancy

Oberlin had old buildings, old trees, and a beautiful campus. It also had a history of being a part of the Underground Railroad during Civil War times. Bicycles were everywhere. Few students, except some of the married students, had automobiles. Everyone walked or rode bicycles to classes and the housing units that served the meals. Outside of town there was a small beer joint that was popular with the students. One of the local drug stores still had an old fashioned soda fountain that was also a student favorite. My sister was particularly fond of the lime sodas when she was at Oberlin. I think my favorite was the hot fudge sundae.

I had enrolled in a pre-med program so many of my courses were pretty much predetermined. There were some slots open for electives and I really enjoyed some psychology classes, art history, and comparative religion studies in addition to my required classes. Unfortunately I demonstrated my ineptitude for language studies and did not do well in either French or German. One of my very best friends at Oberlin was Eb Evans. We were both WWII veterans. He had dealt with explosives and had had a few close calls which left him with some lung damage but he seemed generally to be in good health. We both were interested in photography and had both done a fair amount of darkroom work. In those days almost all photography was black and white and processing required working with smelly chemicals in a darkroom which usually had very little ventilation. Before long we found that we were the college newspaper's two photographers. This was a fun assignment but it took far too much of our time that should have been used for studying. We covered all major events for news photographs and spent long hours at night processing our pictures in order to meet printing deadlines. In those

Oberlin Transportation

days we had no computers so all processing had to be done in the darkroom or by actually cutting and pasting our finished prints in order to make montages. Once you are known for your photographic capabilities you are in great demand to take pictures for all sorts of groups and individuals and most people don't have a clue as to the time involved, so it is easy to get sucked in to time consuming ventures that nobody wants to compensate you for. I'm sure I should have declined that job and spent more time studying – this was not the only time I made bad judgments concerning priorities and time allocation. We sometimes got started on bridge games in the evening and some games went all through the night and into the morning when it would have been far more prudent to get some sleep or do some studying.

There were all sorts of extra curricular activities on campus. I enjoyed some of the intramural sports activities such as touch football. I was quite quick and coordinated but not big or muscular so I would have been a total bust at college football, but I was really pretty good at non-tackle football. I also started noticing some of the ladies. Oberlin was not a place to be for the proverbial dumb blonde – pretty girls were also bright. I became quite enamored with Chrys Jensen. She was from Melba, Idaho and her father ran a big ranching operation. He was still running sheep at the time. Chrys was a very strong girl who had helped work the ranch and she was taking a physical education program. One time we were walking back to our dorms after lunch when one of the boys in the group started playing sort of rough and was really starting to annoy Chrys. When he didn't stop as she requested, and got rougher instead, she decided to end the harassment and gave him a quick jab to the ribs. He immediately stopped the roughhousing, turned pale, and went to the infirmary with a broken rib. That was my first realization that ranch girls from the West were pretty self sufficient. We were beginning to get somewhat serious before I

33

realized that my goals of medical school would not really fit into her plans to return to Idaho and help on the family ranch, so I encouraged my best friend Eb to pursue Chrys when I decided to leave Oberlin and transfer to Wisconsin after two years. Because of the overcrowding, the class scheduling was such that it would have taken me at least an extra year to complete my pre-med program at Oberlin. After I left Oberlin, Eb and Chrys got married and years later when I moved to

Vale and Ontario I located them in Boise and saw them on rare occasions over the years. Eb had taken over the family ranch and did well in the cattle business. Unfortunately both

Studied Hard - Mere Shadow of Self

Dorin & (Clockwise)-Chrys,Barb,Gerry,Joy - Great Folks

of them have died in the past few years. They were wonderful people.

Bert Lahr in "Burlesque" - Detroit, Michigan February 1948

One weekend I was able to get to Detroit, Michigan with some friends and we were able to see a stage show, *Burlesque*, with Bert Lahr, famous for his role as the Cowardly Lion in the *Wizard of Oz*. For photo buffs this picture was taken with a small folding pocket camera with an f2.8 lens using ½ frame 127mm film – probably using tri-X film. The picture was taken hand held with stage lighting only.

One summer I, along with a couple of other Oberlin students from Wisconsin, took a summer job as counselor at Red Arrow Camp near Woodruff, Wisconsin. In addition to being in charge of a cabin full of boys I was the archery instructor, camp photographer, and photography instructor. I was also assigned to a job for which I was totally unqualified. Apparently because I was in a pre-med program in college they thought I could act as camp doctor – wrong-wrong-wrong. In essence I became sort of a first aid person but definitely was not capable of making medical decisions. Fortunately we didn't have any serious medical problems that year. This was the first job where I needed a Social Security number so I had to apply before I could get paid. I was invited back for the next year but other things came up when I transferred back to the University of Wisconsin the following year.

After World War II my dad had returned to the University of Wisconsin and became the chairman of the Department of Chemistry, where he channeled his energies into solar energy. Although phasing out of nuclear energy he still consulted in both fields for quite some time. He became world-famous in solar energy and physical chemistry, as well as geochemistry and thermoluminescence, later becoming president of the American Chemical Society, of Sigma Xi and the Geochemical Society, and was active all his scientific life in AAAS. He was elected to the American Philosophical Society and National Academy of Sciences where he was one of the Vice-Presidents for several years. He made many around the world trips on lecture tours, usually taking my mother with him. She wrote up many of their travels in detailed letters which provided a very interesting chronicle of their activities. In spite of my father's fame and titles he never failed to be courteous or respectful to everyone around him. As an example of his concern for others I recall that Lee Henke, the machinist in charge of the machine shop at the chemistry building for many years, suffered a severe stroke which left him unable to speak coherently, and what words came out tended to be vulgar and filled with profanity. Lee had helped my father on many research projects. He was to my knowledge essentially uneducated, but he had the uncanny ability to convert my father's ideas into workable devices to be used in his research projects. After his stroke Lee was too disabled to return to work. In spite of his inability to converse, and the discomfort that my father had with his language (my father abhorred profanity), my father visited this tragically disabled man at his home on a regular basis. I think this represents my father's respect for all individuals, regardless of their title or degree.

Back at Madison for my last two years of college at the University of Wisconsin, I stayed at home part of the time. I joined the Alpha Delta Phi fraternity and lived at the fraternity for awhile, the newest of the Daniels family line to join. My great-grandfather John Horton Daniels had been a member at Hamilton College in New York State in 1845. His brother-in-law was also a member at Hamilton. His son, my grandfather, Franc Birchard Daniels became a member at Hamilton in 1871. His brother was also a member. My father Farrington Daniels became a member at the University of Minnesota in 1910. My father's two brothers also joined at Minnesota. My brother Farrington Daniels Jr. became a member at Wisconsin in 1940 and my cousin John Horton Daniels Jr. joined at Minnesota in 1949. At the fraternity I was music director for awhile and we had a chorus that I directed. I found that there were too many distractions at the fraternity, and while the Alpha Delta Phi fraternity was much more academically oriented than many I still found it difficult to study so I moved to an apartment for awhile. Sometimes I would spend several days at home to get more studying done. For transportation I acquired an old 1935 Chevrolet sedan for $170 from the husband of our previous maid "Linnie." The car was in fairly good mechanical shape but was cosmetically challenged. Parts of the fenders were missing, there was almost no upholstery and you could see the road through the floor boards. The engine and tires were OK. The battery was pretty weak and I would park the car across the street on the hill so I could coast down the hill in the morning to get it started. I did what I could to make the car presentable but for quite awhile I couldn't afford a new battery. I would frequently take my dad to work in the morning when I was staying at home so mother could keep the family car.

One of the summers while I was back at Madison going to the University my dad and Professor Emmons from the Geology Department teamed up on a research project. They got a grant for a project that turned out to be dual purpose. At that time in the post-war era there was great concern about the possibility of a war with Russia. During this Cold War there was a great push to find uranium. Dad was interested in peacetime uses of atomic energy and Dr. Emmons was interested in the mechanics of uranium deposition and the formation of the uranium ore. The two of them had collaborated on several possible theories. My dad had also started some studies on thermoluminescence. He had already established that many rocks with some crystalline structures would give off light when heated. From his studies he was able to demonstrate that x-rays or other ionizing radiation would recharge those rocks after they had been heated. He had found that in areas of increased background radiation, such as near uranium deposits, there would be increased amounts of thermoluminescence, so the two studies were related. To make a long story shorter the two professors decided to take a trip into Canada, around Lake Superior, studying rock formations in and near known uranium deposits. They

Canadian Float Plane We Used To Go To Uranium Mine

arranged for me to go along as an unpaid helper whose job was to drive the University car, set up camps and be the camp cook in remote areas, and assist in the experiments. Almost everywhere we stopped Dad would chip rocks and heat them in a device which measured the amount of light emitted. We also took many Geiger counter measurements. One day we went to a lake where it had been arranged for us to fly by float plane to a remote uranium mine so that we could study the area. What an experience it was to be involved with two scientists who were evolving theories as we went. While driving I was trying to absorb as much of the back seat conversation as possible. On that trip Dr Emmons developed a new theory of uranium deposition based on the geological formations that we found at new prospecting finds and the chemistry of uranium that my father was familiar with. Also on that trip we were able to further the explanation of thermoluminescence which was later used in the technique of dating pottery from archeological excavations as well as the development of dosimeters to replace film badges for x-ray technicians. What an absolutely wonderful experience to be involved with cutting edge discoveries.

The last two years at Wisconsin were fairly uneventful. I had finally learned to concentrate more on my studies and spend less time on extra curricular activities. One rather interesting incident occurred in one of my English classes. A rather abrasive lady instructor was quoting my father (my father had been instrumental in establishing a course at the University called "Contemporary Trends" which had become quite popular so his name was well known on campus even outside of the Chemistry Department) and she referred to him as J. Farrington Daniels. After she repeatedly referred to him as J. Farrington Daniels I raised my hand and commented that his name was Farrington Daniels without any "J." She seemed annoyed at my comments and insisted that I was wrong. After some further discussion I finally told her that I thought I should know, because he was my father. She stopped arguing but seemed rather upset that I had corrected her and I think I got a slightly lower grade in that class than I was expecting.

In general I got reasonably good grades at the University of Wisconsin but not enough to make up for my rather dismal earlier record, so I was pretty discouraged about my chances of getting into medical school.

My father had heard of an opening at the biologic division at the Oak Ridge National Lab where he knew many of the people, so I applied for the job and took a few extra genetics classes in preparation.

Oberlin Winter Scene

OAK RIDGE and ENIWETOK

My Bachelor of Science degree from the University of Wisconsin and the extra genetics courses gave me the credentials needed to be hired at Oak Ridge National Laboratory in 1950. I had to go through a rather elaborate and extensive FBI investigation to get a Q clearance in order to work at Oak Ridge. Fortunately I did not have any difficulty, but it was a close call because at the University of Wisconsin there had been some communist front student organizations, which were not necessarily identified as communist. Some of these organizations had tried to get me to become a member, but as I was not particularly anxious to be involved in a lot of activities I did not join, and had I done so I certainly would have been denied employment at Oak Ridge. I went to Oak Ridge in the summer of 1950 as soon as my clearance was approved and I started working with Dr. Alan Conger in preparation for the Eniwetok bomb test experiments. Also working in the laboratory was a bacteriologist's assistant named Kathryn Meyer who went by the nickname of "Toddy" and I was

DANIELS
DORIN S
CIV ORNL

Badge Photo

quite smitten. We had a whirlwind romance and soon announced our upcoming marriage to our folks. My mother was both surprised and pleased because she was quite status conscious, and some of my previous girlfriends had not quite passed muster with her. Toddy was the daughter of a professor and that seemed to make things a lot better for my mother.

We were married on December 8, 1950 and in January I departed for

Toddy Wedding Announcement Photo

Eniwetok Atoll in the Marshall Islands located in the central Pacific Ocean. My job at Oak Ridge was to work on *Tradescantia* which is a plant that has large chromosomes which are easy to study. Our projects with those chromosomes were to study the radiation effects on direct hits to the chromosomes with various types of radiation. We did studies with alpha and beta rays, x-rays and gamma rays of various intensities, and neutrons. We were able to calibrate in the lab what doses we were exposing the plants

39

to. We were able to count the chromosome aberrations as the results of the radiation affect, categorize the type of deformity, and draw curves of dose versus biologic effect. The purpose of this was to develop a biologic dosimeter system so that we could compare the mixed radiation of the atomic bomb to the physical dosimeters that we had used in the lab. So actually I was hired as a male technician to take our plants out to Eniwetok, to be exposed to the atomic bomb blasts. There were to be several blasts in this series which I believe were being developed in preparation for the trigger of the hydrogen bomb which was to follow. Thus we had several atomic bomb blasts in which to enter our biologic material.

Our biomedical unit with its personnel and experimental supplies was placed on the small island of Japtan which was one of the forty islets making up the Eniwetok Atoll. The larger island of Eniwetok was pretty much blasted flat in the war with only stubs of coconut trees left. We were across a narrow water strait from the island of Parry which was next to Eniwetok. Our island of Japtan was essentially intact and was a little tropical island with coconut trees and a native population of large lizards. It had actually been used as a military recreation site towards the end of World War II. In the middle of the island they had cut out some of the trees to make a baseball field, but other than that the mess hall, barracks, and laboratory buildings were all pretty much inside of coconut groves and were shaded.

The planners of the operation looked over a sketch of the site and noticed that one of the laboratory buildings had a little greenhouse attached, which was to be used to hold our biologic materials. They actually used our little greenhouse as the code name of the entire operation: Operation Greenhouse. During our preparations for the bomb blasts one of my duties was to water the plants and keep them healthy. One morning, at the time I was usually out caring for the *Tradescantia* plants, I had been allowed to read some of the classified plans for the total operation and I found it fascinating, so I was a bit late tending the plants. While I was reading this very fascinating material I heard a small plane with the engine sounding funny and some other noises which didn't sound normal. When I finally realized that there was a plane in trouble I started out the door toward my greenhouse, which was only about three feet away, just as the small plane crashed into it. If I had actually been where I should have been I would have suffered a direct hit. It turns out that the small plane, which was a little spotter observation type plane, was dropping the mail sack into the baseball field, which they did on a daily basis. On this occasion the pilot got too low and got shielded from the prevailing wind, losing some of his lift, and he couldn't power out in time to get above the tree line. He hit trees and what I had been hearing were the fluctuating engine noise and the noise of trees being chopped up by the propeller. The pilot was seriously injured, was airlifted to Hawaii, and died a few days later.

I will always remember the comments of one of the doctors in our group who had been a flight surgeon in World War II. He had previously complained bitterly and repeatedly to the powers that be that these small spotter observation planes had a design flaw that needed to be corrected. The safety harnesses were attached to the seat, and the seat was only anchored to the floor with a few bolts or rivets. There had been a history of fatal crashes which should have been nonfatal crashes. I remember this physician officer being very upset, as he was the first on the scene of the accident and quickly assessed the pilot's injuries, and told us that statistically this man was dead because of his injuries. Any one of his injuries would probably have been survivable but the combination was too overwhelming. This doctor felt that the injuries would have been very survivable if there had been adequately placed shoulder harnesses. I remembered his comments very vividly as years went by and I became a pilot, a pilot medical examiner, an FAA crash investigator, and an assistant county medical examiner.

We lost some of our plants in that plane crash, but it wasn't enough to stop us from proceeding with our experiments. We did have to get more plants shipped over but because there were several tests several weeks apart we were able to keep functioning. Dr Conger died many years after this incident and while I was reading his obituary in a genetics journal I noted that the author commented that Dr. Conger had been very lucky, because his assistant had been killed when a plane crashed into his greenhouse at Eniwetok. I was the assistant and feel fortunate that the author was misinformed. I tried to find the author to tell him that it was the pilot who died and the assistant was OK but I never was able to locate him.

The bomb tests themselves were quite an experience. I believe our island was approximately seventeen miles from the actual bomb blasts.

The bombs were placed on towers and various experiments were done including structural integrity tests with houses and factory-like buildings. The biological materials used consisted of our plants, dogs, pigs, mice and other materials placed at varying distances from ground zero with various types of protective material. The pigs were used for thermal burn studies and they were placed in lead canisters with only small windows as a means of studying skin flash burns without a lot of radiation affect to the whole body. Dogs were used for various experiments primarily related to radiation poisoning and LD50 studies. LD50 is the term used for the dose at which 50% of the animals died. There was some concern that the anti-vivisectionists in the Hearst newspapers would hear of our experiments and make a big fuss about dogs being used for experiments in which some died.

I was high enough up on the totem pole to be issued very dark glasses. Enlisted men and other supporting nonscientific people were not issued glasses and were required to hunker down and look away from the bomb as it went off. Those of us who were issued the extremely dark welding-type glasses found that they were so dark that even in the middle of the day we could barely see the outline of the sun. At daybreak, when most of the tests were scheduled, we would watch the bomb go off and even wearing our glasses the sky lit up to extremely bright levels, almost painfully bright, and far brighter than the daylight would be without the glasses. After what seemed like an eternity of the fireball ascending to great heights, building and building and building, we wondered if some of the theoretical concerns of a chain reaction going through the atmosphere might actually be a reality. As the brightness faded over many minutes and got to the point that we could barely see we took our glasses off and it was again far brighter than daylight.

As soon as the blast and fireball had settled down pretty much to nothing, and the cloud had started to dissipate down wind, we got into our landing craft and were taken by the sailors who operated those craft to the island to retrieve our material. We were issued canvas booties, old worn out combat boots, worn out combat fatigues, masks, and gloves, and were put ashore as the first team because we had biologic material that needed to be retrieved and brought back to the laboratory for ongoing analysis. The structural and other tests did not require the immediacy that our biologic material required, so we were actually first on the scene. On one of our retrieval trips, after a blast, I found some playing cards near some of our material. I don't know if

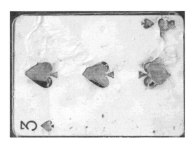

Flash Burn Effect - Atomic Bomb - Eniwetok

that was part of an official experiment, or somebody's unofficial action, but I did pick up one card as a souvenir. This card was an excellent demonstration of flash burn effect with the white of the card's face unaffected and the black markings burned out. I had a friend at the lab in Oak Ridge place the card in plastic for me when I got home, and I still have that memento.

After we retrieved our material we would take off our protective clothing and put it in a trash barrel for disposal. We did wear film badges (used to measure radiation exposure) and apparently none of us got any serious exposure. On one of the tests, the Navy man who was running our landing craft was pretty much incapacitated. He was thin, and he was emotionally drained, and I think he probably was still suffering World War II combat fatigue, or perhaps a thyroid problem. At any rate he was having difficulty keeping himself organized, and though I had no sea experience, I had been in the Navy and I pretty much took over the boat on that trip. Fortunately all went well. I believe the sailor needed and hopefully got some psychiatric help as he was definitely not functioning well. I saw several of these blasts go off and was returned to Oak Ridge before the last one in the series went off, which I believe was the first hydrogen bomb but I'm not sure.

When we had some slack time between tests Dr Conger introduced me to snorkeling. We were able to obtain snorkel tubes and flippers for our feet, and whenever we had a chance, we would spend several hours exploring the coral reefs, watching the sea life and looking for shells. On a few occasions we had to swim very hard to get across tide channels. Fairly frequently we would peer around a piece of coral and see a 7-10 foot shark looking at us. We were told that these were sand sharks and were not likely to cause us any trouble, but they still gave us a bit of a thrill. On one occasion Dr. Conger was able to arrange for us to be taken by boat and dropped off at a very tiny island that had not been frequented. This allowed us to see some of the reef that had not been damaged by other swimmers. The brightly colored fish, the eels, the sharks and absolutely huge clams (approximately three feet in diameter) were truly amazing. During some of those trips I was able to

43

collect some nice shells for my father-in-law who had a fine collection from all around the world. On one of our snorkeling trips Dr Conger was stung by a Portuguese Man of War and he had a quite severe allergic-type reaction which made it difficult for him to get back across the tide channel. I was not really aware of the degree of distress he was suffering until we were actually back on shore and he was able to get some medical attention. He had a close call and if he had not been able to get prompt attention it could have been quite serious.

My boss at Oak Ridge and at Eniwetok, Alan Conger, was a geneticist and a fine man. I was hired to be his assistant primarily because they were not taking any female assistants to Eniwetok. The only females that ever showed up at Eniwetok apparently were an occasional nurse flying through on military flights. Dr Conger had been a student in Hawaii at the time of the outbreak of World War II. He was up on the hillside on the island of Oahu when the Japanese struck Pearl Harbor, so he witnessed the attack and actually had shell fragments landing near him. After the war he became a geneticist and went to work at Oak Ridge. The overall director of the biomedical program was Dr. George LeRoy, who at the time of these tests was a medical officer at the Hines Veteran's Hospital near Chicago. Dr. LeRoy had been in World War II as an Army medical officer, and was in the first team of American medical doctors to go into Japan after Hiroshima and Nagasaki were bombed, and the war was over. So within a relatively few days of the attacks on Hiroshima and Nagasaki Dr. LeRoy was in the bombed areas, seeing the effects of radiation, as well as the bomb blast, on many civilians. He was one of a very few doctors to have had any experience with radiation exposure in a wartime setting. (The names of Alan Conger and George LeRoy should be remembered because they play a part in the naming of our second child.)

I was gone a few months and when I came back in the spring of 1951 I was pretty much used to the climate of Eniwetok which was semi-tropical because of the vast amount of ocean surrounding the Atoll. We had military flights from the west coast all the way to and from Eniwetok. Dr. Conger had arranged for us to have a two or three day layover in Honolulu, which was not common, but he wanted to visit old friends he had not seen since the beginning of the war. He borrowed a friend's car and we toured the island and I saw things I would never have seen on my own. After I returned to the states I got a flight back home to Oak Ridge via Knoxville, with an overnight stay in Madison to visit my folks and just about froze to death as my body thermostat was used to the unwavering 70 plus degree temperature, and here I was in a Wisconsin spring.

Alan Conger In Hawaii On Way Back From Eniwetok 1961

After I got back to Oak Ridge Dr. Conger and I spent several months finishing up our calculations with the *Tradescantia* experiments. We had made numerous slides of the biologic material and were now finishing the analysis. When the studies were done, and Dr. Conger no longer needed me for that particular job, I worked for several months as an assistant to Dr J. Kirby Smith who was doing other radiation studies.

When I got back from Eniwetok, Toddy and I were able to move into our new apartment. We had been living with Toddy's folks before my Eniwetok trip while new apartments were being built and we were on the waiting list. Toddy lived with her sister in Oak Ridge for most of the time I was gone. During our off time at Oak Ridge we took quite a few trips to various places in Tennessee and once to Florida where Toddy's folks had a vacation home on the island of Captiva. Toddy had

Toddy and Dorin Visit Oak Ridge Apartment Approx 45 Yrs Later

been a member of The Smoky Mountain Hiking Club for many years so I joined the club and we had some nice hikes with fine people. During my last winter at Oak Ridge I joined a basketball team. There was a league competition throughout the entire Oak Ridge National Laboratory and our biologic division was a very small unit compared to most of the other divisions. Members of our division joined the league to have fun and to get some exercise, and really had no expectations of being really competitive. We had one member who was quite tall but who could not see well through his thick glasses, a few pretty good athletes, several pretty enthusiastic non-athletes, and short little me who had shot baskets at my childhood chum's house. Probably because we were just having fun we surprised everyone and did quite well, and actually won the league championship.

Later on, in 1951, after Dr. Conger and I had finished the Eniwetok reports, Dr. LeRoy stopped by my office at Oak Ridge, put his feet up on my desk and asked me what I planned to do, well aware that I would not have much of a future at Oak Ridge without a Master's degree, or more preferably a Ph.D. I told Dr. LeRoy that I had always wanted to go to medical school, and that was what I still wanted to do but had doubts that I could get in. He questioned me further, asking if I had applied to any medical schools, and I said yes. He asked which medical schools I had applied to and I told him three or four that I had applied to that I thought I might have a chance at, but I was pretty discouraged as to my prospects. He wondered why I was not expecting to get into medical school. I told him I was not a straight A student, and there were so many returning veterans finishing their educations who wanted to go on to medical school that the competition was extremely tough. He responded that grades weren't everything, and had I considered applying to University of Chicago. I said "No, their standards are so high I don't even think it's worth applying, there's just no chance." He said, "Well, your father was there at the Metallurgical Lab working on the Manhattan Project and you've been in research, and they're pretty high on research at the University of Chicago." I responded "Yes, but, it's not my dad's grades that they're looking at." He again said, "Well, grades aren't everything - you apply to the University of Chicago and I'll be glad to write you a letter of recommendation." I said "Well okay, I'll do it but I still don't think there's a chance." He again said "You apply!" and as he walked out the door he turned around and looked back at me and he said, "Oh, by the way, I am leaving the Hines VA Hospital and I'm going to become the Assistant Dean at the University of Chicago Medical School." Well, sometimes it's a matter of who you know! He wrote his letter of recommendation and I don't remember the exact wording so I'm paraphrasing, but he started off with a statement sort of like this – "I lived on a desert island with this man for a few months and I believe I can attest to his character," and then he went on to describe my

46

experience in scientific research and my family background, so it was a surprise to me but I was accepted to University of Chicago.

Our firstborn child was delivered in Oak Ridge on February 26, 1952. His name was Donald Farrington. Toddy's family had a foster child whose name was Donald and she wanted to name our firstborn Donald because she was so attached to the child she helped bring up. The middle name Farrington (a family name) was for my brother and my father who shared the first name Farrington. When I went to Chicago and the second child came along on October 16, 1953 while I was in medical school, he was named Alan, for my boss Alan Conger and middle name LeRoy for Dr. LeRoy who was the director of the biomedical program in Eniwetok, and who was so helpful in getting me into the University of Chicago medical school. I finished out at Oak Ridge in the spring of 1952 and left in time to take a summer school correspondence course that I needed for admission to medical school. We spent the summer before medical school in Madison living with my folks and spending some time at the cabin in Door County, and then medical school started.

Donald - 3 mo - Oak Ridge

Alan - 3 months - Chicago

Toddy's Childhood Home - Fountain City, Tennessee (Knoxville)

Medical School

We arrived at The University of Chicago Medical School in time for orientation for the class of '56 and to get into our housing unit. Prior to WWII there were almost no married students in medical schools. Schools of Medicine and Schools of Nursing historically had admission requirements of being single. They had felt that the schooling was too rigorous and time consuming to allow the distractions of marriage. After WWII the schools had to adapt to the fact that many of the applicants who had served in military service were already married and many also had children. The school had a block of small WWII flimsy prefab houses south of the Midway across from the University. These flimsy cracker boxes were available for married students and were always filled. They had almost nothing resembling insulation, were heated with oil, the smelly barrels placed next to the front porch where they were easy for fuel trucks to fill. Most of us with children were very happy to have a place of our own – we actually had a tiny yard that the kids could play in and we were glad not to be in an upstairs apartment. The wives and mothers in the compound soon developed new friends which was necessary for their sanity because most saw little of their husbands for long periods of time.

Alan and Don in Chicago Yard Pool

For the students the pace was very demanding. The amount of material covered in the first two years of medical school was incredible. There were many absolutely brilliant students in my class, including several who later became noted in various aspects of the field of medicine. We had a large variety of backgrounds in our class. Many came from academic or medical families. Some came from very difficult circumstances like Z. S. Hruben who had been trained in medicine in a Russian occupied country and escaped from the Russians by actually crawling under a barbed wire fence and dodging machine gun fire. He seldom talked about his ordeals but on one occasion I asked him if he thought the Soviet Union and its oppression would last very long. He thought the oppression was so severe that it could last for about one

49

hundred years before it would be overthrown. He was a brilliant student and stayed in academic medicine in Chicago for many years.

Donald Steiner was in my class and he stayed in academic medicine and became world famous for his research in diabetes.

Edmond Jacobs had been a fighter pilot in WWII and had gotten into trouble on a couple of occasions – once while on a night training flight he had turned on his landing light while flying low over a long straight stretch of railroad track directly toward an oncoming train. The terrified railroad engineer tried to make a panic stop because he was sure he was on a collision course with another train on the single track. It was said that the train had some flat spots on its wheels after that incident. Another time he was flying at night when a flare fell from his plane, setting off a big explosion in an ammunition dump. He was headed for severe punishment until a mechanic was able to prove that the flare release mechanism on his plane was defective and that the situation was really an accident. Edmond was considered sort of strange and far out for his conviction that we would send people to the moon in a fairly short period of time and that he wanted to be in the first group to go into space. (Our class started in 1952 and President Kennedy didn't make his famous speech about going to the moon until 1961.) I don't think Edmond made it into the later-formed NASA program, but he was far more right about the coming space programs than we gave him credit for.

Bill Odell was a very personable and outgoing classmate. He and his wife Margie had several children and sometimes our children would play with theirs. Bill started doing research in Charles Huggins' lab quite early in medical school. (Dr. Huggins was a professor who later won a Nobel Prize for his surgical work in endocrinology.) One time in our junior year we were making class rounds on Dr. Huggins patients and Dr. Huggins was telling a patient what he planned to do surgically for him in a day or two. He asked the patient if he had any questions before agreeing to the procedure. The patient thought a minute and said he would need to discuss it with "his doctor", while pointing to Bill, the student who had seen him on admission the previous night, before he would agree to any surgery with the professor. We held our breaths but Dr Huggins seemed to enjoy the situation and just smiled. Bill later became chief of medicine at the University of Utah.

Many other classmates became noted in their fields. Several became professors. Keith Kelly became chief of surgery at the Mayo

Clinic branch in Scottsdale, Arizona. Several classmates became psychiatrists which was a bit surprising to me as psychiatry was not a strong program at the University of Chicago at the time we were enrolled. Another surprise that I didn't learn about till I attended my 50th graduation reunion (the only reunion that I ever attended) was that several of my classmates actually entered general/family practice and some of those became professors, as did I, while teaching family practice medicine via preceptor programs. The University of Chicago had actively discouraged general practice while strongly pushing for academic medicine, research, or super specialization. I lost track of most of my classmates but they were an outstanding group.

The first two years of medical school were brutal. Classes were fast paced and tough. We would start in the early morning with classes and labs and there was essentially no time for relaxation. We frequently had evening conferences and had to study late into the night. Anatomy lab in the freshman year was spent dissecting cadavers, and with four students for each cadaver, we worked as teams. I was never good at memorization so I jumped at the chance the next year to be an instructor in the anatomy lab helping the next class. I guess I took a cue from my dad who always said that the best way to learn something well was to teach it or write a book about it. In the 1920's he realized that mathematics was becoming more and more essential in his field of Physical Chemistry, and that he felt somewhat weak in the subject, so his solution was to write a book on "Mathematical Preparation for Physical Chemistry." That book was in print until calculators and computers took over from slide rules in doing calculations. It had one of the longest printing runs (over 35 years) for any text book ever published. I learned more anatomy the year I was instructing than I did the year I was a student, but I never felt that I had mastered the subject.

We had a quarter system at Chicago and the fall quarter would finish up with final exams shortly before Christmas. In order to give me more uninterrupted study time Toddy took the kids by train to Knoxville to visit with her folks and her sister's family while I was getting ready for exams. After exams I drove to Tennessee, joining them for some vacation time before we all drove back to Chicago.

In our third year we were seeing patients in the hospital. One quarter we were assigned to the medical wards, one quarter to the surgical wards, and a third quarter we were assigned to the obstetrical service. We had to work up every admission on our service and we had to draw the blood and do the basic blood and urine studies on everyone. In those days we did not have the rapid "dipstick" tests that are common today so the lab tests were tedious and time consuming. We had to make the blood smears, do the differential counts, hemoglobin and hematocrit tests, red cell counts and white cell counts. Special chemistry tests like blood sugars, sodium levels, etc were sent to the lab. Urine testing required fairly time consuming procedures that now are done in a minute or two with "dipsticks." To test for albumin in the urine we had to boil the urine. This created a very unpleasant smell that permeated the hallways. The lab work that we were required to do typically took more than a half an hour for each patient and we would frequently have four or five new patients arriving after supper. By the time we finished doing histories and physicals as well as the lab work on these new patients it would often be midnight or later before we got home. We would then have to be at the hospital at seven a.m. to present the patient's history and physical findings to the attending physician while on rounds.

We, like most of the other married students, were living on a shoestring. Some of us had GI Bill benefits left that had not been totally used up in college. We had saved one salary while both of us were working but it wasn't enough to keep us going very long. Most of us had to get student loans to stay in school. Toddy had become an excellent shopper and knew which stores to go to for canned goods, or produce, or meat. Powdered milk was very inexpensive at that time

Grandpa Farrington Daniels Visits Us in Chicago - 1953

and our boys didn't get regular milk for many years; when they were introduced to regular milk, or even 2% milk, they thought it was sort of slimy. On a rare occasion on weekends we would splurge and get a pizza and some ice cream and drive to a nearby yacht harbor where we would picnic on the shore and watch the expensive boats come and go. My father was still consulting on both nuclear and solar energy and he was also on business trips for the American Chemical Society so he came through Chicago fairly often. Occasionally he would be able to stop by and visit for a short time. He

52

had an uncanny ability to show up for a visit about the time we were down our last five or ten dollars and many times he saved us in the nick of time with a check for $50 or $100. I don't know how he could have been so psychic as to seem to know when we were getting desperate.

One time we were invited to dinner at the home of Harold Urey, the Nobel Prize winner, who was a friend of my father. Unfortunately it was one of those rare evenings when one of the boys was totally out of sorts and was totally inconsolable. The Ureys were very nice and very understanding but we were never invited back. I suspect that we should have sprung for a baby sitter that time.

On a few occasions we were able to get away for several days and vacation at the cabin in Wisconsin. We could get to the cabin in a one day drive and a sometimes we were able to stop at Sheboygan on our way to Door County and visit with Toddy's Aunt Florence and Uncle Herb Schultz. Florence was my father-in-law's sister and her husband owned chains of grocery stores named "Piggly Wiggly" and "Schultz-Savo." They were gracious hosts and usually fed us when we stopped by. Toddy would usually go to his warehouse and pick out a bunch of groceries for our trip. After the bill was tallied and paid, Uncle Herb would usually ask her if we needed something like lobster tails, or steaks, or something else that was totally out of our financial reach, and after Toddy sputtered for awhile he would throw something special into our cart and refused our attempts to pay for it. Herb was legally blind from retinal detachments that I think resulted from football injuries but he still drove his car much to the consternation of friends, family, and police. He actually had fairly good vision in a very tiny field of view so he would drive with his head cocked at a peculiar angle. Everyone who rode with him was petrified because he couldn't see anything to the side of his limited forward vision. Those who recognized his car would give him a wide berth. Herb raised excellent hunting dogs and had them trained for show and competition and had many a trophy to show for his achievements. Unfortunately, many years later his house burned and most of the trophies were lost. They had a lovely house in Sheboygan which had a nice swimming pool that our kids loved. We enjoyed stopping by to visit them over many years.

I don't know how we finagled enough time for a trip between quarters but in early September of 1955 we managed to take a long trip through the western United States to look at possible places to apply for internship. There was, and still is, a matching program nationwide that provided a mechanism for senior medical students to be picked for internship slots. Senior students would list their top several choices in order of preference and the institutions would list their top choices of students, also in order of preference, from those who had applied. In March there was a "Matching Day" when all of the information was tabulated and students were assigned to internship positions. This matching program would have been a simple task with modern computers but as we had none in those days it was quite a lengthy and tedious process. My dean of students had tried to convince me that going west was not a good idea and suggested that I stay at Chicago or try for Johns Hopkins or some other top eastern institution, or if I really felt I needed to go west he thought it might be OK to go as far as the University of Colorado at Denver. My friend and advisor Dr. LeRoy was much more supportive. He said I could learn a lot from a good internship but could also learn a lot about what not to do in a really bad internship. When I told the Dean of Students, Dr. Ceithaml, that I planned to go into general practice in a small town somewhere in the west he was visibly distressed. In spite of the fact that I was a struggling student, and not near the top of the class, he thought I should stay in academic medicine, or research, or at least become a specialist. When he realized that I was actually serious he acted like he had failed in his duties. He was actually a very good dean of students but he thought his students should be above general practice.

We had already come to the conclusion that our Ford sedan, which I bought new for $1500 when I finished college, was getting pretty small for our expanding family. Toddy had fallen in love with the advertisements about the newly introduced Volkswagen Microbus, and had said something to her mother about it. Just before our western trip she worked out a deal with her mother to buy the VW Bus with her mother's money and how we were to pay her back later. There was no other way we could have bought anything at all for another several years without that help. That VW was a godsend. It was great for our needs and we rearranged the seats and made some modifications so that Toddy and I and the two boys could sleep in the bus. An early porta-potty and a gas stove allowed us to camp along the way no matter where we went. We sold our Ford to a classmate. By that time we had hand painted the badly faded maroon color to a green color that wasn't as pretty as we thought it should be. We had found a kit so that we could lower the back of the front seat to make a bed, and we had put in a rebuilt engine because the block had cracked. I saw Ed Kolner, my classmate who bought the car, years later and he said they got many years of good use from that ugly old hand painted car. When we started our trip west we joined my sister, Mino, and her husband Marty who had a new Chevrolet and had been spending some time at the Cabin. We would travel at different speeds because our VW was a bit underpowered with 36 horses but we would meet along the way by chance or by prearrangement. We had no cell phones or radios with which to communicate in those days but we managed to meet at a good place to spend the night. We left from Madison before Mino and Marty and planned to meet later in the day because we had Toddy's mother with us and were planning to drop her off at Merrimac, Wisconsin to visit with her sister (maybe it was a cousin) before heading up the road into Minnesota. The first night we found a nice campground at Albert Lea in Minnesota. We fell into a pretty smooth routine which worked well for the entire trip. I would set up the stove and get the VW ready for the night while Toddy started supper and Mino watched the kids. Marty would set

Setting Up Camp on Trip West - 1955

up their tent and after eating Mino would do dishes while Marty blew up air mattresses and Toddy and I tried to get the kids to bed. The second night we made it to Volga, South Dakota where we dropped in, unannounced, on the Alonzo Peeke family. They welcomed us warmly and invited us to stay the night. Alonzo, or Lonnie as he was called, was a cousin of my mother. Dr. Peeke was an excellent family doctor who was loved by his community. He did quite a bit of surgery and apparently did it well. He took me to see his "hospital," a converted house with an operating room and a few beds that could be used if someone needed to stay overnight. He lamented the fact that inspectors were threatening to shut his hospital because he did not meet new "standards." What seemed to upset him the most was that he didn't meet the requirements for knee or foot operated controls at the scrub sink where he washed his hands before surgery. Apparently the government inspectors didn't buy his claims that he had been washing his hands before surgery for many years and he knew not to touch the faucet handles after washing. He had routinely had his nurse turn off the faucet when he was done but that wasn't good enough for the inspectors. I didn't fully understand his frustration for a few years until I saw first-hand the steady encroachment of externally mandated regulations.

When we left in the morning our destination was the Stratosphere Bowl where the famous balloon flights took place taking man higher than man had ever gone before. The Stratosphere Bowl in the Black Hills was on private land and not open to tourists but a classmate of mine, Richard Daniels (no relation), had made arrangements for us to visit. He had relatives living there and they had been forewarned of our arrival. From there we went to Mt Rushmore, the Big Horns, Yellowstone National Park, the Grand Tetons, Boise, Idaho, and on to

Alan, Dorin, Toddy, Don, Marty (Mino's Husband) - Trip West 1955

Mino and Marty's apartment in Corvallis, Oregon. We stayed in Corvallis a few days while I investigated some internship possibilities in Portland and Eugene, Oregon. When we left Corvallis we headed south and checked some possibilities in the San Francisco Bay area. From there I don't recall the route we took home but at least I had seen several internship programs and was beginning to form some ideas concerning plans for the coming years. Somewhere on that trip we had stopped for gas and I had opened the rear engine compartment to check the oil when an overweight man came running across the street and breathlessly asked if the engine I was looking at was the air conditioner. VW Buses were not common yet and the small engine did not look very powerful considering the fairly large box it was pushing.

In the fall of 1955, near the end of the second quarter of my last year of medical school at The University of Chicago, I was called in to the office of Dr. George LeRoy, assistant dean of the medical school. Dr. LeRoy had been advising me, encouraging me, reprimanding me, pushing me, and supervising a research project that I had started, so I didn't know what was in store for me on this visit. I had known him ever since the Eniwetok days so in spite of being a bit intimidated by his position I knew that he was always my friend. He sat me down and asked how my research project was going. I had started a research project with lung tumor prone mice and was trying to determine if increased oxygen levels would have any effect on tumor statistics. I had been working part time on this research project for some time setting up the lab, obtaining a particular strain of mice, calibrating monitoring equipment, and doing some trial runs. I was planning to put almost full time into the project during my upcoming elective quarter. I told him that I had experienced some trouble keeping the cages at stable increased oxygen levels but that my trial runs so far had not produced any statistically significant variations from normal. He then asked me if I would like to go to Alaska. I replied "Yes, I've always wanted to go to Alaska but I don't have any money and I have two more quarters before graduation," and I asked what he had in mind. He told me that the school had a program for one senior student who had an elective and an off quarter in sequence (i.e. a six month block of time) in which the student would spend six months in a TB hospital in Seward, Alaska working with Dr. Francis Phillips, a thoracic surgeon. He informed me that the hospital, Seward Sanatorium, was run by Methodist women who acquired the hospital from the military (it was a WWII military barracks hospital) and converted it to a tuberculosis hospital. He further informed me that the hospital would provide air fare for the family and give us a modest monthly living expense. Wow! I couldn't believe what I had heard. He gave me long enough to check with my wife before committing but it sure sounded great. I went right home and asked Toddy if she wanted to go to Alaska. She thought I had lost my mind but became more interested when I told her about the program. When she asked when we would have to leave I told her we would have to be in Alaska the first of the year and she about lost it. We had been gearing for a fairly relaxed quarter of research followed by a fairly lengthy vacation before starting internship but this opportunity was just too good to pass up.

On short notice we shipped some of our belongings to my brother's house in Portland, Oregon, where I hoped to get my internship. We packed everything else into our VW bus and started west at the end of my classes. Dr. LeRoy signed off my research with the conclusion that I had done enough preliminary work to pretty much disprove that moderately increased oxygen levels would have a statistically significant effect on tumor incidence in the strain of tumor-prone mice I was working with. My research was to have tested several levels of oxygen saturation but the Alaska experience looked to be much more exciting than three months in the mouse lab. It was almost Christmas time when we got away in our VW bus and headed for Oregon with two kids and lots of stuff including a parakeet that we were going to leave with my sister in Corvallis. This was before the interstate highways were in place so many of the highways were two lane and fairly slow going. With low horsepower (36 hp) and a large surface area our VW Microbus was slowed down by headwinds. The last day before we got to Portland we stopped at the Frost Motel in Ontario, Oregon. We were all tired and the boys were hungry and fussy. We asked the motel manager where we could eat and he directed us to the Palomino Restaurant. When we finished eating it was dark and as we came out of the restaurant we noted that a men's clothing store across the street was still open. Toddy commented that we had left on such short notice that she did not have a winter jacket adequate for Alaska so we went into the store which had the name Toggery Bill's. She didn't care if it was a men's or women's coat so while she was shopping I started visiting with the clerk and casually asked him if he knew of any place that might be looking for a doctor in a few years. He asked why I had asked and when I told him that I was finishing medical school and would be looking for a place to practice in a few years, he immediately started to sell me on coming to Vale when I finished my training. The clerk happened to be Winston Quisenberry, the owner of Toggery Bill's and Quisenberry's store in Ontario, Vale Supply in Vale, and several stores in other towns. We bought a jacket and went back to the motel. That chance meeting had a big impact on my future life. The next day we took the long drive to Portland and joined my brother and sister for our Christmas vacation. Over the next few days we arranged to have our VW bus placed on a barge to be shipped from Seattle to Seward, Alaska, and arranged to get to the Seattle airport in time for our flight headed for Anchorage.

58

Alaska

We landed at Anchorage, Alaska, in the middle of a huge snowstorm. Planes from Seattle that were ten minutes behind us were turned back, but we had passed our "point of no return" and had been directed to the Elmendorf Air Force base because the regular international airport could not keep up with the snowfall. I have forgotten how many years it had been since they had experienced this severe a storm but I think it was something like twenty. The Cold War was still a concern and we feared the possibility of war with Russia, so the military tried desperately to keep Elmendorf open. We literally landed behind a snowplow. Air Force personnel helped carry the two boys and our luggage off the plane, which was a four engine propeller-driven airliner. (Probably a Boeing DC-4 or DC-6) When we got inside a building we learned that most roads were closed and that the town had pretty much ground to a halt. Newspapers and radio stations were telling everyone that the highway to Seward was officially closed. We tried to call Dr. Phillips at Seward to get instructions because we knew we would not be driving that day. No one seemed to know where he was but it was thought that he had left for Anchorage to pick us up. Knowing that he would not be able to pick us up that day we got a cab, one of the few that were able to function, and checked into a hotel expecting that he would find some way to get word to us. As we were leaving our room to get something to eat we bumped into Dr. Phillips. He had driven all the way from Seward on roads that were officially closed and had gone off the road about four times but somehow he made it through. The next morning he said "Let's go" and put us in his early model Jeep Station Wagon in spite of the persistent warnings that the road to Seward was closed. That early model was basically a WWII type jeep with a box on the back. The heating system was not adequate but at least it was a 4 wheel drive rig and he had chains on all four wheels. Our trip to Seward (something like 120 miles) was harrowing to say the least. For most of the trip there was no real clue as to where the edge of the road was and in many places if you misjudged you could roll for many hundreds of feet. Furthermore, if we had gone off the road we wouldn't be found for days because the roads were officially closed and not even the snow plows were going through. Dr. Phillips said he knew the road pretty well and kept charging along.

When the situation wasn't totally terrifying he told me some of the history of the Seward Sanatorium where I would be spending my next six months. It was an old WWII army barracks hospital that had been put up very early in the war to serve the military that were guarding the Seward Harbor. There was great fear early in the war that Japan was going to invade Alaska, and Seward was a very important seaport where ships could come into a sheltered harbor and unload onto the Alaska Railroad for rail shipment to Anchorage and Fairbanks. After the war was over the Methodist women's organization negotiated to acquire the facility to use as a tuberculosis hospital. Alaska had a real problem with tuberculosis and every year the territory's public health nurses would go deeper into the interior and bush country to find new, and frequently far advanced, cases of TB in the Indian and Eskimo populations and bring them in for treatment. (Alaska did not become a state until 1959 and I was there in 1956.) There were no roads in the interior so transportation was by boat, dogsled, and airplane. Dr Phillips was, I believe, the only Board Certified Thoracic Surgeon in Alaska at the time and he was doing innovative surgery on advanced cases of TB. He informed me on this nightmarish trip that he had severe arthritis and had difficulty getting around the hospital so I would be expected to do the daily rounds and he would help if I had a problem. He also informed me that I was expected to do all of the deliveries. I felt that my training was way too inadequate to do deliveries as I had no experience in that line other than observation but I didn't say anything. I was by this time really beginning to wonder what I was getting into for the next six months. I already knew that it would be a wild ride and an experience like no other.

Somehow, miraculously, we arrived in Seward and were dropped off at our new house. The hospital staff had cleaned the house, put out blankets and towels, and had supplied enough food to hold us for a day or two until we could get to the store. They checked us out on the oil furnace and told us why there was a

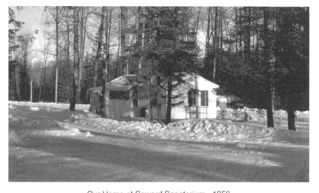

Our Home at Seward Sanatorium - 1956

bag of salt in the bathroom – we were to pour salt down the tub drain just as the last of the bath water was draining out because if we didn't the drain would immediately freeze and it was a real pain to get it thawed. The house was small but tidy and was nicer than the cracker box we had been living in at Chicago. It had a small kitchen, a bathroom with a tub (my wife was ecstatic as she liked tub baths and for the last 3½ years we only had a shower), a fairly small but very adequate bedroom and a very small utility room which served well as a bedroom for the two small boys parked in a double-decker bed. (There was no way you could have gotten into the room if there had been two beds on the floor.) The house was equipped with an intercom that tied me in to Dr. Phillips home and to the hospital. While we were still unpacking I got a call from Dr. Phillips asking me to come to the hospital. I assumed that he was going to show me around the hospital, but no – I was about to be introduced to Alaska medicine! Dr Phillips

Seward Sanatorium During Long Winter Night - 1956

ran a small private practice in his hospital office and this being a holiday (New Years) a lady had arrived at the office complaining of a severe toothache and had not been able to find a dentist. I think she was expecting to get some pain pills to hold her over, but this was Alaska and Dr Phillips looked in her mouth and found a real mess. She had lost all but a few teeth and those remaining were in bad shape. He took her into the dental wing of the old WWII hospital and rummaged around in the still neatly arranged drawers of military dental tools. This woman was terrified of dentists, which is why her teeth were so bad, but she was hurting so severely that she was willing to submit to almost anything. Dr. Phillips found some Novocain to inject and then found dental pliers that seemed to be a good fit for the hurting tooth and pulled it out. The lady was so pleased that the extraction went smoothly that she said "This other tooth (pointing to one) has been bothering me too – can you take it out?" Long story short – she wound up with all of her snags of teeth being removed and she was one happy lady. Dr. Phillips was a Thoracic Surgeon and I was a medical student – neither of us had any

61

dental training – but this was Alaska and you did what you needed to do.

The next day I started into the routine. Actually there was never a routine – everyday could be a new challenge. I made daily rounds on patients, we regularly reviewed x-rays, and one day every couple of weeks we did about a dozen bronchoscope procedures. In those days we had no fiber optic instruments, only rigid bronchoscopes. I was taught the procedure and had the usual novice ineptitude and did a few "incidental" gastroscopies much to the glee of the hospital staff. You have to align the patient in just the right position for the straight and rigid scope (think sword swallowing) to go down properly and in the darkened room the nurses could see the light from the end of the scope through the skin as it slid down the throat and into the stomach if I missed the trachea. Often when doing the bronchoscopy we would insert a catheter down the scope and inject radiological dye into the patient's bronchus, roll the patient around and take him/her to the x-ray department to get some extremely good bronchograms. We had a few pregnant patients and I was continuing to be nervous about doing my first delivery but when the time came I had such great support from the old pro nurses that it went quite well. Those nurses were fabulous – they had seen almost everything that you might expect and then some. I think that if a student, or even a new doctor, had any thoughts that nurses were beneath them instead of being partners they might have had a pretty rough time. When the babies were delivered they were held up for the mothers to see but the mothers could not hold them because of their infectious disease. The babies were taken to the city hospital until arrangements could be made for the public health nurses to take them back to the mother's village where someone would care for the baby. Transportation in the winter was by dogsled and airplane. (There weren't many snowmobiles in 1956.) In the summer it was likely to be airplane and boat. I bet those public health nurses had some wild stories to tell.

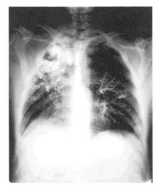

Bronchgram - Bad Lung Disease

Dr. Phillips did surgery on some of his private patients and I helped him with appendectomies and gall bladder surgery or anything else that came along. We would store up necessary but elective surgeries until we could get an anesthesiologist from the Air Force hospital in Anchorage to help us on weekends. At times when we did not have an anesthesiologist we would do thoracoplasties under local anesthesia. This required incredible amounts of local anesthesia and must have been a miserable experience for the patients. Our native patients were very tolerant and stoic and almost never complained. We did a few rib resection thoracoplasties creating major disfigurement and we did several less disfiguring lung collapse procedures with a technique where we kept the lung collapsed by putting large amounts of paraffin in the chest cavity. It was not unusual for us to do twelve or more major chest cases in a weekend when we had anesthesia coverage. We did segmental lung resections, lobectomies, and even a few pneumonectomies (removal of one entire side of the lung) on severely diseased lungs. Post op management kept us pretty busy after these long surgical weekends.

One weekend after about three long cases we took a lunch break and I commented that I didn't feel well. I went home (about 100 yards from the hospital) for lunch and said something to my wife. She looked at me and commented, "Gee, you sure have a lot of pimples today!" With sudden suspicion she pulled up my shirt and there it was – I had come down with a full blown case of chicken pox. I thought I had had the disease as a child but a phone call to my mother revealed that she also initially thought I had the disease but on further recollection she remembered that my siblings had all had chicken pox when I was brought home from the hospital as a newborn and that I never got it. We had only recently been relaxing about a small epidemic in the hospital pediatrics ward where we had a new patient break out with a rash which had the nurses a bit worried because some characteristics of small pox were suspected, and until we had typical cases of chicken pox about two weeks later we were a bit nervous. I came down with the disease in the third wave. I was really sick and my wife knew it when I didn't even want to look at the cartoons in the *Saturday Evening Post*. Our boys came down with chicken pox a couple of weeks later and they sailed right through without a problem.

Occasionally Dr Phillips would insist that I get a bit of a break from the hospital and would encourage me to take the family on a sight-seeing trip or a picnic or whatever we wanted to do to have a change of scenery. One weekend we took our VW Bus, which was set up so we could sleep in it, and drove to Kenai and Homer and camped on a beach where there were fishermen who had come from all over the world to fish the King Salmon run. We couldn't afford a fishing license but it was fun to watch the anglers pull in those very large fish. The road to Homer had only been in place for a few years. Previously,

access to that side of the Kenai Peninsula had been by boat or airplane only. The quaint Old Russian village of Ninilchik with its chapel was very photogenic and I got a few nice pictures on that trip.

VW Bus at Homer, Alaska Sign - 1956

Speaking of fishing, while we couldn't afford a fishing license we were allowed to fish for Dolly Varden without a license. At that time in the Territory of Alaska the Dolly Varden were considered trash fish because they ate some of the salmon eggs. While we couldn't fish for salmon we would occasionally find a big King Salmon stuck in a snow bank by our porch where some hospital employee had deposited their catch to help our food budget. I also took a few short trips to photograph the fabulous scenery. I did some black and white photography and I had a Canon 35mm camera which was a Leica copy with a rangefinder that I used for color slides. (Actually I had essentially stolen the camera from my father after he had picked it up

Milepost 14 Seward Highway - 1956

in Japan and hadn't figured out how to use it and was trying to force the mechanism - so I like to think I saved the camera from destruction.) The color film I used was Kodachrome with a film speed of 12. I got some very nice slides and years later when I brought them out to review I was horrified because most of them were covered with a fungus. I thought I had lost them completely until I found a photographic archival cleaning fluid (PEC-12) that cleaned them up and saved the day. Fortunately, I had used Kodachrome instead of another color film as the colors have not faded in over 50 years.

One weekend I was covering the hospital while Dr. Phillips was out of town. I heard a knock at my door. And there was a hospital employee and he looked distressed. I asked him what I could do for him and he responded with a tremor in his voice that "It's my dog. You've gotta help me." It appeared that his dog had been the loser in an encounter with a porcupine and was in really bad shape. The dog's owner had tried to remove the quills and the dog had been pretty good for awhile but it had become obvious that the dog would have to be sedated before much more could be done. I told the man that I wasn't a veterinarian, and actually wasn't a doctor yet, and that I had no license to practice any form of medicine. He listened but let me know that the dog meant everything to him; it was his friend, his hunting partner, and his constant companion. He insisted that I help him even though he knew I wasn't licensed. I checked the dog and discovered that several quills were very close to the eyes and there were many deep in his mouth. If we didn't get the quills out fairly promptly it was likely that the dog would loose at least one eye or at least suffer starvation. For those who don't know about porcupine quills, they are barbed on the end and gradually work their way in deeper. The poor dog was miserable so I told the owner that I had anesthetized dogs in the dog lab at school but I wasn't real confident of my abilities for anesthesia. The owner told me to do whatever I could, he would trust me and would accept whatever happened, but would I please do something. I went to the operating room, got some Pentothal, and spent some time trying to figure the dosage because all the information I had was about humans and not about dogs. With a bit of apprehension I gave the dog an intraperitoneal injection of the Pentothal and the dog went to sleep. Both the dog's owner and I went to work to remove the mess of quills and just as we were about done the dog started waking up. I was ecstatic that the dog survived, and the owner was delighted that we had gotten the quills out. The owner was so happy that he was trying to pay me. I told him I wasn't licensed in medicine or anything else and couldn't take any money. He finally stuffed a bill in my pocket and told me not to put my hand in my pocket until he was gone. He was extremely grateful for my help. Actually that was my first fee for service even though it was probably illegal. The next day when Dr Phillips, the head nurse, and the hospital administrator were back in town I was called in to the office where I got a lecture about my unauthorized use of supplies. I was reminded that I did not have permission to get anything from the narcotics locker, and that I had violated all sorts of regulations. The voice and message were strong and I really got a dressing down. Through it all I sensed from body language that I was really being told "Good job!" They all were trying to suppress smiles and had twinkles in their eyes that they couldn't hide. They threatened to charge me for the Pentothal and needles and syringes that I had taken from surgery but they never did. In a close-knit place like the Seward San word gets around in the blink of an eye and it seemed like everyone I saw for the next few days gave me a special smile.

I learned a lot about cultural differences during my Alaska experience. Our hospital had a population ratio of about 1/3 Eskimo, 1/3 Native Indian, and about 1/3 Aleut. At first I had trouble telling the Indians from the Eskimos but it didn't take long to sort that out. The Indians tended to be thinner and quieter and the Eskimos tended to be a bit plumper and jollier, and before long I began to notice some facial features that were fairly distinctive. Most spoke little or no English when they arrived at the hospital and most picked up some very limited English after they had been there awhile. Many could not communicate with each other and frequently those who lived in villages fairly close to each other did not speak the same dialects. Almost all of the native population were very accepting of their situation and were appreciative of the help they were getting. One Eskimo girl in her early twenty's stood out. I think her name was Mary and everyone in the hospital loved her. She was beautiful, she was obviously very bright, and she was very happy in spite of having quite advanced TB. She also had the incredible ability to translate for almost any patient. It appeared that she could spend some time with a new patient and before long was able to communicate to some degree. She was constantly in demand to help with communication problems all over the hospital. The entire hospital staff wanted to chip in and help send this talented girl to college when her medical condition would allow. Mary's TB was not getting better on the medicines we had then (streptomycin and the newer Isoniazide) and she was taken to surgery. Surgery seemed to go well and by all parameters that we could measure she was doing OK post operatively but on the second or third day after surgery she calmly announced that she was going to die. She did not seem perturbed or apprehensive, and we could not find anything on physical exam or from the lab tests that we could do that gave us great concern. She did die and everyone in the hospital, both patients and staff, were devastated. There wasn't a dry eye in the

66

hospital for many days. I had a few elderly patients who also calmly announced that they were going to die even though we had no clinical suggestion of deterioration. When these natives said they were going to die you had best believe them. Death to them was nothing to fear and they accepted it with calm dignity. Once they made that announcement they were usually gone within a day or two and never showed any apprehension or fear. They frequently were so stoic that they did not give any indication of pain – even the ladies in labor didn't give any sign of pain and when they called for a nurse and said something in broken English like – "baby come now" you had best be moving fast if you wanted to get them to the delivery room.

As I was getting near the end of my time in Seward I was in surgery one day and the circulating nurse asked me to turn around for a moment. She carefully pinned a piece of gauze on to my surgical cap and said nothing. A little while later Dr. Phillips looked up at the clock and announced "It's about time" and the circulating nurse reached from behind and flipped the piece of gauze from one side of my cap to the other and said "You just graduated – welcome Doctor!" That was my graduation ceremony. They knew when the graduation ceremony was going on in Chicago and I didn't have a clue. After that surgery we took a short coffee break and they had a cake made up so we could all celebrate.

Graduation Day in Surgery at Seward San

My six months in Alaska were absolutely fantastic. I learned a lot about surgery and all sorts of medical problems. I had a real head start on what was to come.

In the middle of June in 1956 we left Seward to start our long drive down the Alaska Highway on our trip to Portland, Oregon where I was to start my Internship at St. Vincent Hospital on July 1. Our trip on the Alaska Highway presented us with some more great scenery. We tried to camp in old gravel pits which were open and not as infested with mosquitoes as the regular campgrounds. The highway was all gravel at that time and most of it was bad washboard. As we got closer to "civilization" we had to do some re-education of the boys. When we got to where there were cattle on the farms we had to teach the boys that they were not moose. (We had moose walking through our yard frequently at Seward.) We also had to stop one of the boys from heading for mile post zero of the Alaska Highway at Dawson Creek to water the tree. For several days prior whenever we stopped driving the boys had been in the habit of heading for the nearest tree. We continued through British Columbia and down the Frazier River canyon where we met some relatives for a night of camping and then made our way to Portland, Oregon. Toddy was pregnant with twins and hospitals were few and far between so I sure was glad that we had not had any serious problems along the way.

Don & Alan at Milepost O - Dawson Creek 1956

Seward Sanatorium Icicles - 1956

Portland - Internship and Residency

We arrived in Portland several days before the internship was to start. My brother and his family were living there so we had a place to stay before getting settled in at St. Vincent Hospital. The old St. Vincent Hospital was on N.W. Westover Rd and was sort of backed into the hillside. It had been there for many years. There were some intern and resident quarters that single persons stayed in but some of us had families and had to find places to live which would be close to the hospital. I don't know how we lucked into it but the hospital owned a BIG house just a few doors around the corner and up the hill from the hospital and they offered to put us in that house for a ridiculously low rent of something like $70 per month. They wanted someone to live in the house and they were only paying me $200 per month so they knew I couldn't afford what would have been a fair market price of perhaps $600-800 per month even in 1956. They had acquired the house because they thought

Our Big Portland Home on NW Westover Road

they might expand and need the ground. (Years later they moved over the hill to the west and built a large new hospital in the Cedar Hills area instead of expanding the old hospital.) One of the reasons I picked St. Vincent was that they actually paid something to their house staff. At that time many of the supposedly prime internships around the country provided board and room only, plus a small uniform allowance but no salary.

We had shipped what belongings we had to my brother's house in Portland when we headed for Alaska and now we had a place to put our meager belongings. We had a couple of beds, a few chairs, a refrigerator, a dining room table, a couple of dressers, and some kitchen utensils. We expanded our furniture gradually by getting a few second hand items and a card table or two and made bookshelves and other storage items out of orange crates. Orange crates, for those too young to remember them, were boxes made from thin wide slats of wood and were used to ship oranges all over the country. Many houses had adapted the crates for some storage purpose or another and they could usually be picked up at the grocery stores for free. Our house looked pretty empty for a long time as our meager household belongings didn't begin to fill that large house with a basement, a main floor, and bedrooms in the upstairs floor, plus an attic. There was a large porch outside around much of the main floor. Some of the posts and railings on the porch were in poor repair but the house was basically in good condition. We built a darkroom in the basement bathroom so I could continue some photography. N.W. Westover Rd. made a tight turn as it climbed the hill and it came back behind us much higher than it was in the front of the house. The hill was very steep and we had no garage so we had to park the VW Bus either way below the house in the street in front or way up high behind the house in back. Front or back there was a lot of climbing to do when we brought groceries or kids in from the car.

Internship was busy. Again we faced long and irregular hours. We didn't have to do much lab work on patients like we did in medical school but we had to work up all admissions. Most of the patients were admitted by their own private physicians but we did have some indigent patients that were cared for entirely by the house staff with back-up from some of the private doctors. While we were not a medical school affiliated institution we had a lot of doctors on staff that held medical school positions. Some of the medical school professors brought their private patients to St. Vincent hospital so I felt that we had top notch instruction. Many of the doctors on the hospital staff were solo doctors and some were from small clinic groups, but the staff appeared to be dominated by the Portland Clinic which was a large and influential group and they used St. Vincent Hospital for the majority of their admissions. Most of the doctors were very good but I was beginning to notice that some definitely used better judgment than others. In my intern class most were very good but I could see that they did not always approach problems in the same way and some were not able to "multi-task" (a term that came into use in the computer age and was not used much in 1956) worth a darn. I remember seeing one of my intern classmates, while on an emergency rotation, sitting in a corner of the emergency room doing a slow workup on a patient with a minor problem while a person with a severe emergency was ignored – this new doctor absolutely could not function without finishing one problem before starting the next. Even though I was not on that service I stepped in and with the help of some others got things going to help that injured patient. I obviously had a jump start on most of the others because of my Alaska experience but I was more timid about doing new things than many of the others. Most of the members of the attending staff were very helpful and some were absolutely superb teachers.

One of those great teachers was J. Oppie McCall, an OB/GYN specialist who had a great reputation for dealing with complicated pregnancies. We had chosen him to deliver our twins because of his reputation. We had suspected that Toddy had an abnormal pregnancy while still in Alaska. She had shown excessive uterine growth and we had taken an x-ray before leaving Alaska and had noted twins. Furthermore, one twin did not appear to have a normal head but we weren't sure if this was just from motion or a real deformity. We didn't want to take more x-rays but we were definitely concerned and were glad to come under the care of Dr. McCall. When it came to teaching, Dr. McCall was very hands on. He spent hours on the obstetrical service working with interns and residents showing them how to use forceps in a variety of situations. He used the baby/pelvis manikin and walked us through many abnormal as well as normal presentations with and without forceps. His training was invaluable to me in later years. When it came time for Toddy to deliver our fears were realized – the first twin delivered had a congenital condition called anencephaly (a condition incompatible with life) but fortunately the second twin, Kathy, was born small but normal on September 21, 1956. When the first twin expired a few hours after birth we elected to donate the baby to the anatomy lab at the medical school to use as a teaching specimen, much to the consternation of the nuns who thought it should have a "proper burial." I didn't realize how important it was to the Catholic sisters that the body be placed underground. We assured them that sometime, maybe hundreds of years later, the baby would be underground and they were partially pacified.

It seems strange in the current era but when I started internship the closed chest massage and cardiopulmonary resuscitation (CPR) as we know it today had not been developed. We would have spirited discussions with others on the house staff as to how to decide when, and on whom, to slash the chest open and manually massage the heart with our bare hands. There had been a few dramatic saves reported but those were rare and the overall success with open chest cardiac massage was pretty dismal. We had worries that if we tried to save someone under some emergency situations that observers might mistake our actions as murderous intent. We also knew that if the patient's heart started up again and we were in an out-of-hospital setting, we would have continuing problems with the pneumothorax that we had created, bleeding from the chest wound, and almost certain infection. We all carried pocket knives but hoped we would never have to face a decision of "slash" or "no slash."

I had excellent training on many services and was allowed considerable freedom to arrange my schedule during my residency year. I concentrated as much time as possible on surgical, obstetrical, and pediatric services but also got a broad coverage of medical services.

One time while I was on the obstetrical service I got a panic call from home. Our obstetrical call schedule was 24 hours on and 24 hours off which we liked because when we were off we were really off. When I got the panic call I was in a busy period and there was no way that I could quickly get home to help my wife who was frantic. Apparently Alan, our three year old second child, had gotten up early and while Toddy was still sleeping had started painting in the kitchen pantry – a job that had been started the night before. Apparently when he finished in the pantry, including all of the cans he could reach on the shelf, he decided to paint the banister on the stairs. He appeared at Toddy's bedside with paint dripping off his arms and asked her to help him open another can of paint. Fortunately it was water based paint but Toddy had a bad day and it was several hours before I was able to help her clean up the mess.

One of the real perks that the residents had once we had obtained our license to practice medicine (we could apply to take the examination as we were nearing the end of our internship) was to be the doctor at local high school football games. Some of the junior varsity games were held in the afternoons and if we got to cover those games we could actually get outside in daylight and breathe some fresh air. In addition we were actually paid something for our services. This was great! On one of my first football games I felt a bit unsure of my role and was tying to enjoy the game when one of the quarterbacks was hit hard and was dazed. I checked him on the sidelines and I thought he had suffered a mild concussion and shouldn't return to the game. Apparently the coach felt that the boy wasn't hurt bad enough to stay out of the game and kept pushing me to let him back on the field. I held my ground and said I would check him more extensively at half time. The boy had a foul mouth but I had no way of knowing if that was out of character for him. I did as much of a neurological evaluation as I could in the locker room at half time and found nothing really alarming but I still felt uncomfortable. As the second half started the coach was getting more and more impatient with me to let the boy play. I finally relented with qualifications. I would allow the injured quarterback to go back in the game with the understanding that he was to come out and stay out if there was even the slightest sign of trouble. On the first play after entering the game the quarterback took the ball from the center, turned around as if for a hand off and holding the ball himself immediately ran back over his own goal line. The pushy coach meekly pulled him out and didn't give me any guff for the rest of the game. I saw the boy later in the evening at the hospital where he was brought for continuing concussion symptoms. He was much improved in a couple of days and even his speech became more civil.

I seldom had any time off but on a few occasions the family was able to get away for a weekend. We managed to get to the Oregon beaches

Joining Brother and His Family on Oregon Beach c. 1956

with my brother and sister's families on rare occasions and we drove to Crater Lake with some of my intern classmates once. In my second year when I was a resident we spent a few weekends traveling around the state looking for possible places to practice. As we were starting the process of looking for a place to practice we had several considerations, one of which was that our oldest son, Don, was having some asthma problems and it was thought that he might do better in a dryer climate. For that reason one of the places we considered was the Vale-Ontario area and I called Mr. Quisenberry. Mr. Quisenberry was the clothing store owner that we met by chance a few years earlier on our way to Alaska. When I had him on the phone I identified myself as Dorin Daniels and asked if he remembered me. His immediate response was "Hell yes! When are you coming?" A brief conversation indeed but we put a visit to Vale on our schedule.

When I was able to get away for a weekend we went to visit Vale. Mr. Quisenberry was most helpful and took us around town and gave me a real Chamber of Commerce-type introduction to the town and had me meet some of the people. Vale had recovered from a rather devastating and fairly recent flood and had shown civic pride in cleaning up and it looked quite clean. The county seat was in Vale even though Ontario was larger and more the business center of the county. When we got back to Portland we decided that Vale was where we would move and start a practice. As I started doing the required paper work to start a practice I ran into a few snags. At that time you were required to be a member in good standing of the local county medical society in your area in order to start practicing. I wrote repeatedly and got no answer from my request to join the society. I was beginning to get concerned that I might not be able to get started when planned. One day Peggy, the hospital switchboard lady who acted as chief mother hen for the house staff, informed me that Dr. Joe Burdic from Ontario was going to be at a meeting in the hospital. She knew that I was planning to practice in that area and suggested I look him up. Joe had taken an internship at St. Vincent hospital a few years earlier and was coming to an education meeting. I looked Joe up at the meeting and told him of my dilemma and concern about joining the Malheur County Medical Society. After a brief visit he calmed me down and simply stated – "we're pretty relaxed out our way – consider yourself a member." I had seen Portland doctors work and scramble hard to climb in the ranks of the local society and I thought I was going to like the "relaxed" atmosphere of Malheur County.

Kathy at 10 Weeks - Portland

Vale

We arrived in Vale, Oregon, in the latter part of June 1958, having finished a one-year residency in General Practice following a one-year general internship at the old St. Vincent Hospital in Portland, Oregon. It was our intent to set up our house and make some final arrangements for an office, arrange for supplies to be brought into the office, and then take a couple of week's vacation. We had not really had a vacation for quite some time and, as I had accumulated some vacation time, we left the residency a couple of weeks early. The normal transition time would have been July 1. We met with Vale realtor, Kenny Johnson, who owned Flying Realty, and he arranged for us to get a house, and also arranged for us to get a loan with the bank. He actually personally loaned us the down payment so that we could get the bank loan. We had nothing except debts at that time, other than a few household belongings. The office that we rented was over the Kessler Chevrolet garage, and it was owned by Dick Humphrey who was a local businessman. Most of these arrangements had been orchestrated by Mr. Quisenberry who owned Vale Supply, Toggery Bill's, and Quisenberry's Store in Ontario, and also owned stores in several other cities. He is the one who had tried to attract us to the area a few years before when we were on our way to Alaska. He also introduced me to Carol Evans, who was just out of high school, and he recommended her as being an honest, hard working and trustworthy sort of individual. She was hired as my first office assistant and was the only employee I had to start with. Our plans for a vacation went by the wayside. We had to wait awhile to get into the house, and we stayed in the Bates Motel at the west end of town in the interim. The office needed painting, and some other modifications such as building a darkroom for an x-ray, and so forth. George Hart had been the postmaster in Vale for many years and he also did sign painting on the side so we had him paint my first "shingle" which we put up over the door at the entrance to the office. I still have that "shingle" over the entrance to my study at home. We had to hire some work done but we did the painting

D. S. DANIELS, M.D.
PHYSICIAN & SURGEON

First Shingle - Vale, Oregon 1958

ourselves. When painting the office I realized that it wouldn't take long to get busy as many patients started coming up the steep stairs to the office and asked if I was the new doctor. They then proceeded to tell me what their difficulties were. I did have a black bag at that time, but no office furniture, record keeping system, or business system. I had arranged for hospital privileges, so I could order some lab work, do a few minor procedures at the hospital, and if need be I could admit patients to the hospital.

When we got into our house on West Main Street South, which was a little house with one bathroom, we found that patients would show up on the front lawn, even before we had a telephone, asking for advice and wanting to be treated. Also, shortly after our arrival, the Vale

Rodeo was under way and on several occasions a car would stop in front of the house and dump off an injured cowboy for me to take care of. I still had no equipment and no functioning office, so I would put him in the car, drive him to

Our First House on West Main Street South - Vale, Oregon

the hospital in Ontario (18 miles away), get x-rays and put on casts, then bring him back to deposit him at the rodeo. I learned then that rodeo performers were a different breed – they had a tendency to remove their casts the next day as it got in the way for the next performance. I don't think at that time that I got paid for any of those problems, as I had no functioning office.

I found the street layout in town rather confusing. The main east/west street, frequently referred to as Main Street, or the main drag, was actually A Street. Slightly to the east of the center of town there was a Main Street. West Street is sort of in the middle of town, and west of West Street was W. Main St. South, which is where our house was located. It was a little bit difficult as a newcomer to find my way around town. Of course in those days there were no cell phones, no radios or other means of communication other than plain old telephones. To make it worse, people would call in the middle of the night asking for a house call, and even though they had lived there for many years they couldn't describe to me where they lived. The conversation would go something like this "Hey Doc, my wife is having a heck of a belly ache, can you come over?" to which I would respond, "Okay - where do you live?" I would then get a response like

"Box 213." I would then have to ask again what street they lived on. There was no mail delivery at the time, so everyone went to the post office to get their mail, and they all knew their post office box number, but frequently they didn't know their street address. If the caller still had trouble remembering his street address he would try to help by asking if I knew where John B lived. Apparently everybody in town knew John B and where he lived, and who lived two doors from the caller. The caller seemed as surprised that I didn't know John B, or where he lived, as I was surprised that the caller didn't know his own street address. We would eventually get general directions, and the best advice was to tell them to turn on the porch light in order to help me find the right house.

Gradually my supplies arrived. In my last few months in Portland I had spent several days looking for equipment that I would need, working with medical supply houses, and Shaw Surgical Supply was the one that was most helpful. They had a branch office in Boise, Idaho, and they assured me that I would have local service from there, so I bought the basic office supplies that I needed from them. I also went to various x-ray supply houses in Portland, looking for an office x-ray machine, and I learned quite a bit about office x-ray units. I also learned something about business practices that I had not encountered previously. Big name x-ray companies had lots of equipment and all sorts of reasons why I should use their product, but as I inspected them and asked more questions and got more information I found that some of the big-name equipment really was not well built. I finally settled on a fairly unknown brand but one that I found to be extremely well built. It was a Profex x-ray and it was built with heavy gauge metal and its wiring was very professionally done. I found very sloppy wiring in some of the big-name companies' equipment and I was not impressed. When I got to Vale and my equipment arrived, I was visited by a GE representative from the Boise area who told me that I had to get my x-ray supplies through him, or else he would run me out of business. I didn't take kindly to that type of threat, and from then on I got my x-ray supplies from other sources. You might recall that I had worked at Oak Ridge National Laboratory and had worked with all types of radiation so I was not as unfamiliar with x-ray technologies as the usual starting doctor.

At the time I started practicing in Vale there were two hospitals in the area. One was a small community hospital in Nyssa, and the other a

Catholic hospital in Ontario. I soon found that some of the patients had strong preferences for one or the other, and I had hospital privileges in both. It did make it somewhat awkward when I had one or two patients in each of the hospitals and would have to make rounds, usually twice a day, in addition to the office practice in Vale. As this became more and more burdensome over the next few years it stimulated my interest in moving to Ontario, which had my primary hospital, as I felt the need of being closer to the hospital, and traveling less. The first few years in Vale were good. I rapidly developed a family practice. I had some very dedicated patients, and I started doing deliveries which I enjoyed, as I had more than the usual experience and training in Obstetrics for a general practitioner. Most of the people going into a general practice at that time had taken only a year of internship, and had a very limited amount of obstetrical exposure, but I had already delivered babies in Alaska while working there in the TB hospital and I had several months of good obstetrical training and experience in Portland where I delivered about 50 babies. At that time the residents were running a maternity clinic for unwed mothers and I delivered quite a few from around the state who had been sent in for care and schooling until they delivered and adopted their children out before returning to their home towns.

It might be of historical interest that, when I started practice, the usual office call was $3, and my first deliveries including prenatal care and delivery was a total of $35. It didn't take very long to realize that I would not make a living wage at those rates, particularly after a year or so when we did some very simple mathematics - dividing my expenses by the number of patient visits and finding that it was costing me on

that very crude arithmetic basis $3.52, and for that I received a $3.00 office call. So, as with all things in life, the price went up, not very high but definitely up. I never became rich, and actually never intended to. I worked long hours and probably if calculating income would have found that I was pretty close to minimum wage

I Had Lots of Pediatric Patients - This is Teresa considering the hours I worked. I kept getting busier and had some very interesting cases over the years.

During my residency in Portland I spent a couple of days per week for several months working in the outpatient surgical clinics at the medical school. This was an invaluable experience in which I was not only seeing and doing a wide variety of out-patient surgical procedures but also I was helping to teach the students some of the surgical techniques. This experience gave me a lot of confidence for doing minor surgical procedures when I started practice in Vale. One of my early surgical successes was on a well known rancher who came to me with a large bump on the top of his head which was somewhat disfiguring and was highly visible on his prematurely balding head. It was a cosmetic problem that was bothering him considerably. I had taken care of many lipomas at the surgical clinics in Portland so I had no hesitation removing the offending lesion, which I did under local anesthesia. I got an excellent cosmetic result and I don't remember what I charged but I suspect it was thirty or forty dollars. Even in those days a plastic surgeon would have charged several hundred dollars to do the same job. Looking back I think that this popular rancher was probably a great advertisement for me, and had I gotten a poor cosmetic result it's likely my whole practice would have been adversely impacted.

When I started practice it was a requirement that you be a member of the local medical society. At that time there were actually two medical associations. One was the Malheur County Medical Society which was supposed to have regular meetings and coordinate with the Oregon Medical Association. The other group was called the Eastern Oregon Medical Society which was a hold-over organization from times past where doctors from La Grande to Jordon Valley came to meet a few times per year for educational and social endeavors. This organization gradually faded out but I was able to attend a few meetings before it totally disappeared. At those few meetings I heard some absolutely fascinating stories from the "old" doctors who were still alive. Old Doc Jones from Jordon Valley told us about some of his ventures such as riding his horse out to a cow camp to take care of a rancher with a broken leg. He would set the leg as best he could and improvise a splint or cast and stay with the wounded patient for several days to be sure everything was going OK before riding his horse back to town. Or Dr. J. J. Sarazin from Nyssa, who would make rounds with his horse and buggy all the way from Nyssa to Juntura and other small towns, a round trip distance of over 150 miles, trying to time his visits with when he expected a lady patient to deliver. He would stay with the family for a week or two until the baby was born. Dr. Sarazin was in no big hurry to switch to automobiles because he could fall asleep in the buggy and the horses would take him home but in a car he would have to stay awake. Another story that J. J. Sarazin told was of going on very bad roads (I think in his first car) to deliver a patient at Watson, a small town up the Owyhee River that was later flooded out when the Owyhee Dam was built. The weather was bad and the roads were very muddy and hard to navigate so he decided to stay a week or so until the baby came. When Dr. Sarazin sent his bill for services rendered he received a bill from the patient's husband for board and room - in the exact same amount as the medical bill. We also heard some wild stories from some of the old Baker City doctors describing their experiences with mining injuries they had cared for. I wish we had had tape recorders then as those stories were priceless and should have been recorded.

It is expected that any new doctor arriving in a smallish town is going to be "tested." All of the hypochondriacs, many who had worn out their welcome with other doctors because they had been wanting too many pain pills, or for some other reason, and some who were just curious to meet the "New Doc" would show up to check me out. I found that many patients were very attached to their doctors in Ontario or Caldwell or Boise but they didn't want to bother them at night or on weekends so they would call me when they needed help on off hours. They would of course go back to their regular doctors during normal working hours. Some patients were never happy and went to every doctor they could find in order to get something magic that their other doctors hadn't been able to provide. There were three old Becker brothers and I think they had seen every doctor in the area. They were well known ranchers from a pioneer family in the Westfall area. They all smoked heavily and they had worked in dusty conditions all their lives. They were also a bit irascible. All of them had bad lung disease and the first one I saw was staying in a motel in Vale. I made a house call on him and found him to be literally gasping for air and he was using an oxygen tank that was cranked up to pretty much a maximum level. While I was trying to get his history and do a physical exam on him he would periodically turn off the oxygen and light a cigarette. When I told him that he had emphysema and that he needed to stop smoking his response was "Hell, you aren't any better that all the other Docs – they've all told me to stop smoking – don't you have anything new?" The only advice he ever followed was to turn off the oxygen while he was smoking. Another early patient that "tested" me was an elderly man in the nursing home. He had been examined by several doctors for a chronic itchy rash. I took a very detailed history and did a thorough skin examination. He kept getting more and more impatient with the time I was taking trying to figure out what his chronic condition actually was and how to treat it. Finally in disgust he blurted out that I must be pretty stupid – he had seen a doctor once who took one quick look and said "I know exactly what you have – it's called dermatitis." Well, there are multitudinous types of "dermatitis" and they don't all respond to the same treatment. I don't think I scored many points with that patient. Early in my practice, actually it was during one of my first two a.m. house calls, I was checking an elderly man who was visiting in the area. He was complaining of chest pain. After I checked him over and visited for awhile I presented a bill. His reaction was "Hell Doc – we can't get a doctor to answer the phone for that amount in California." I guess I hadn't learned how to charge.

The doctors that were in practice in the area when I came to Vale were:

The Ontario Clinic –

Dr. Weese – one of the original founders of the Ontario Clinic who was considered to be one of the early internal medicine specialists.

Dr. Palmer – he had been the main surgeon for the whole area for many years. He had also obtained a radiology certification and had developed skin problems from years of doing fluoroscopic examinations without lead glove protection.

Dr. Emmett – one of the last of the breed of EENT specialists (Eye, Ear, Nose. and Throat). The specialties of "Eye" and "Ear, Nose and Throat" split apart after his training. He, like the others in the Ontario Clinic, did a lot of general practice.

Dr. Belnap – he delivered thousands of babies and was extremely busy delivering most of the babies in the whole area during WWII. He and the above doctors were the early members of the Ontario Clinic.

Dr. Sanders – one of the later additions to the clinic was very busy and delivered a lot of babies until he developed some personal problems. For many years he was the team doctor for the high school and I think he went to most of the games, even the out of town games.

Dr. Sam Pobanz – Sam did general practice but had had some extra training in Pediatrics. At the time I arrived in the area he was considered to be the local pediatrician. He spent lots of time with mothers and was much loved by his patients. He was instrumental in educating the local physicians to do throat cultures to check for strep and certainly he had something to do with the local decline in rheumatic fever. However he did have difficulty facing severe clinical challenges. Sam also directed a local chorus that I sang in for awhile until my wild schedule made my attendance too unreliable.

Dr. Burdic – Joe was one of the younger members of the clinic. He took on a large load of obstetrical patients as Dr. Belnap was phasing down. He had a very busy general practice. He left not long after I arrived to take a psychiatry residency and then returned to the Ontario Clinic as a psychiatrist. For his own sanity he continued to do some general practice even after he had his boards in Psychiatry.

Dr. Lester Scott – he had been briefly in Nyssa as a GP and then some time in the military as a flight surgeon. He joined the Ontario Clinic just a few years before I arrived and even though he was fully trained as a surgeon and was board certified it took many years before he really became busy doing surgery because a lot of patients considered Dr. Palmer to be "Mr. Surgery."

Dr. Delbert Scott – Delbert was a local boy whose father had been a coach at the high school for years. He was a GP at the Ontario Clinic for a few years until he took a residency in pathology and then went to Boise as a pathologist for many years. He and Dr. Miles Thomas, another pathologist in Boise, covered our pathology for many years before we obtained a resident pathologist.

Dr. John Sigurdson – he joined the Ontario Clinic several years later. By the time he arrived as an obstetrical and gynecology specialist I was overwhelmed with deliveries and was very glad to see him arrive.

Other doctors in the area at the time I arrived who were not associated with the Ontario Clinic were:

Dr. John Kopp - Vale. He had been in Vale a few years before I came. He was a good GP. He was a member of the Naval Reserve which took some of his time and he had a string of horses that he took into the mountains for fairly long summer vacations.

Dr. Johnson - Ontario. He was an older doctor when I started practice. I would occasionally see him at hospital staff meetings but he did office practice only and had pretty much given up trying to stay current. At least, to his credit, if he had a difficult case he would refer it to the Ontario Clinic.

Dr. James Flanagan – Dr. Flanagan had taken an internal medicine residency in Detroit and was board certified. He had practiced briefly in a small town in Wisconsin before coming to Ontario and joining the Ontario Clinic. When the Tanaka Clinic building was built he moved in with Drs. Ben and Gus Tanaka. For many years he was the only board certified internist in Malheur County.

Dr. Benjamin Tanaka – Ontario. Ben had an incredible story. He was born in Hawaii of Japanese parents. He had been placed in child labor in the Hawaiian pineapple fields where he was mistreated by the crew boss. He stowed away on a ship and landed in Seattle where he knew no one. I think he was about twelve at the time. He literally knocked on doors and was taken in by a Madame of a house of prostitution who kept him in the basement to keep the coal furnace going and doing other janitorial type jobs. She kept him away from the "occupants" of the house and eventually arranged for him to move somewhere else considered more appropriate for a youngster. After several moves he wound up in Spokane where he worked as a houseboy for a family that helped him get an education. He then worked his way through college and medical school and was in practice in Portland when WWII broke out. Because he was a prominent member of the Japanese community, he and his family were scooped up and placed in relocation centers. He continued to provide medical care to the occupants of the relocation camps for the entire war. He was moved from camp to camp and not allowed to see his family the entire time. After the war he settled in Ontario where the Japanese were better accepted than in many other places.

Augustus (Gus) Tanaka – Ontario. Gus was a son of Ben. Gus had been removed from Reed College when the family was taken abruptly to the relocation centers at the beginning of WWII. After several months he was allowed to continue his education away from the west coast and entered school at Haverford College in Pennsylvania. He was later drafted into the service and sent to the University of Minnesota where he was placed in Japanese language school. (He had been brought up in a bilingual household but had to learn "the ball is red" and "see Spot run" in Japanese.) About that time the war ended and he was sent to Japan in the intelligence service where he experienced the uncomfortable situation of being an Asian in a GI uniform in a country that didn't particularly take kindly to Americans, and surrounded by GIs who had been taught to kill Japanese. Because there wasn't much need for the talents that he had been trained for he was assigned to teach English to illiterate American GI's. After he got out of the service he finished his college and went on to medical school in New York. It was in New York that he met his wife to be, Teddy Wada, who had been brought up on a farm in the Vale area and was then working as a nurse in New York. Gus took a surgical residency in New York and then joined his father in Ontario where he started his surgical practice in 1958 – the same year I started my practice in Vale.

Dr. J. J. Sarazin – Nyssa. Dr. Sarazin had practiced in Nyssa for many years. His stories of horse and buggy medicine were legendary and I wish we had been able to record some of his "old-time" medical stories. Within a few years from the time I started practice in Vale Dr. Sarazin's son David joined him in his medical practice in Nyssa.

Dr. Louie Maulding – Nyssa. Dr. Maulding was a long time doctor in Nyssa before I arrived in Vale. I had little contact with him except at staff meetings at the Nyssa hospital.

Dr. Clay Morgan – Nyssa. Dr. Morgan was from a local family and he was working with Dr. Maulding when I arrived. Clay was a very fine GP who helped me with several patients that I had in the Nyssa Hospital. He was a very good friend of Quentin Quickstad who had been a surgical resident at St. Vincent Hospital in Portland while I was taking my internship and residency there. When Dr. Quickstad finished his residency he and Clay went into partnership and opened a practice in Boise, so Clay did not stay in Nyssa very long. Many years later Dr. Morgan's son Clay Jr. married Barbara Radding who was a teacher and then an astronaut with NASA

Dr. Ken Kerby – Nyssa. Dr. Kerby had been a doctor in WWII. He was not a specialty-trained surgeon but he had a lot of wartime surgical experience and did quite a bit of surgery in Nyssa. He only had one eye having lost the other to surgical removal for a melanoma of the eye.

Dr. Ken Danford. – Nyssa. Dr. Danford was a partner of Dr Kerby doing general practice.

Dr. Grant Hughes – Nyssa. Dr Hughes was a general practitioner in Nyssa. He had had some surgical training but was mostly doing general practice. He was LDS (Mormon) and hinted that he would probably have to leave the area because there were so many Mormons in his practice that expected big discounts that he didn't think he could make a living if he stayed in Nyssa. He moved to Portland and became a psychiatrist.

Dr. Jim Mann – Parma, Idaho. Dr. Mann lived and practiced in Parma, Idaho and utilized hospitals in Nyssa, Oregon and in Caldwell,

Idaho. He became a partner in a Stinson airplane with Tom Gray (a veterinarian) and me. He moved to Ontario and joined the Tanaka Clinic group after I did. He was an excellent family doctor and we shared facilities and personnel at the Tanaka Clinic for many years.

Dr. Richard Woodward – Payette, Idaho. Dick had been in Payette and using the Ontario hospital for many years before I arrived. His father had also been a Payette doctor. He was a general practitioner.

Dr. Tom Watts – Payette, Idaho. Tom had been a Navy patrol plane pilot in WWII searching for enemy submarines off of the eastern coast of the United States. After medical school he joined Dr. Woodward in Payette. Tom and his family joined my family on a few camping trips when both families were playing with trail bikes (small motorcycles.) Tom had a very unfortunate motorcycle accident resulting in a neck injury that left him in chronic pain and enough disability that he had to give up the rigors of general practice. He moved to California and went to work for Kaiser Permanente where he had better working hours.

Dr. Eugene Carroll – Payette, Idaho. Gene got his training in the accelerated wartime programs and was a doctor in WWII. After the war he set up practice in Payette. Years later his son Ron joined him in the practice as did his son-in-law Vernon Barton.

Dr. Kotas – Payette. Dr. Kotas was very quiet. I never really knew him and he didn't stay in the area very long.

Dr. George Davis – New Plymouth, Idaho. Dr. Davis was a long time general practitioner who took care of multiple generations of New Plymouth families.

I may have forgotten a few of the doctors but many of the older doctors mentioned gradually died or retired leaving a fairly small number of active physicians for many years. As the years went by we gradually accumulated a variety of new doctors but for a long time the above doctors were the nucleus of the medical community. When we were getting short on doctors and tried to recruit more physicians to the area we had great difficulty for a long time. Most of the newer graduates were heading for large clinics so they wouldn't have to deal with the "business" side of medicine or they were afraid they couldn't handle a small town family practice. Another reason we had difficulty recruiting was that a high percentage of the wives didn't want to go to small towns. Also, as we later got emergency room physicians and government-supported migrant health clinics, the patients were getting used to the idea that they wouldn't be seeing the same doctor on each visit.

Our children were pressuring us to get a dog for a pet and we finally relented. One of my very fine farm family patients was raising yellow Labrador dogs and we went out to the farm to look at the puppies.

Alan, Don, and Pat (The Owner) - "Pickin Puppies"

These were high quality pups and Don and Alan were given the choice of the litter. The little boy in the farm family had been in my office frequently for a chronic illness and he was considered the owner of the litter. His name was Pat so we named the dog "Pat." Pat was a wonderful dog and we got her fairly close to the time our last child, De Wilda, was born (August 9, 1959). Pat was a very gentle dog and was a good protector and companion for our kids for many years and grew up as a part of the family. When we were camping Pat would stay with the youngest children like a mother hen and if our young ones would pester Pat by putting fingers into Pat's ears or eyes her response was to gently use her paw to move the offending arm – she never snapped or growled at our children. She was hit by a car once and we thought we might lose her. I did a quick exam and took her to the veterinarian who confirmed my diagnosis of hemo-pneumothorax. (Blood in the chest cavity and collapsed lung.) The vet kept her in his hospital for a few days and she pulled through much to our relief.

As the children were getting bigger we needed a larger house. Charlie Fields, a long-time Vale resident, had built a very fine brick house on West Street S. and wanted to move to a smaller home. He convinced us to buy his house and we eagerly moved to the much bigger house. A few years later when we decided to move to Ontario we sold the house to my dentist and friend Bob Keveren. Bob

Second Vale House - West Street South

and his wife Mardene still happily live in that house some forty six years later. Their oldest son Phillip, who I delivered, turned out to be a remarkable person. He was very talented musically and was also accomplished in judo, achieving black belt status. How many people do you know that can go from a judo match to a music competition in the same day? Phillip is not only an accomplished performer in piano and organ but he did a lot of musical arranging in Hollywood, and now is arranging and composing music in Nashville. He is credited with being one of the top arrangers of Christian music. He has produced some absolutely delightful CD's. Phillip's brother John, who I also delivered, also earned a black belt in Judo.

The hospital in Ontario, Holy Rosary Hospital, was larger and had more patients than the Nyssa hospital. At the time I started it was run entirely by the Sisters, and they had actual nuns in charge of almost every floor, the operating room, in anesthesia, in the business office, as the x-ray technician, and as the medical librarian. While these ladies were extremely dedicated, some tended to fall a bit behind on modern medicine. The anesthesia we had from one of the sisters was definitely not up to the standards that the younger surgeons and I had experienced in our training. This made us quite uncomfortable. For the more difficult surgical cases we would frequently take our patients to Nyssa where the hospital administrator was Chuck Smith. Chuck was a newly well-trained and certified nurse anesthetist, and he did an excellent job of anesthesia, with which we felt very comfortable. Several years later Chuck moved to Ontario to become the administrator of Holy Rosary Hospital and continued to do anesthesia.

Vale was not only a hunting and fishing town, it was a school athletic town. The high school teams had been very successful and the football team was on a roll, winning many championships. There were several large families of big, strong farm boys who had some star player on the team almost every year. One of these players was Dave Wilcox. When I attended a football game in Dave's senior year I noted that if the coach pulled him out for even a few plays, to let someone else get some experience, Dave would pace the sidelines like a caged lion and was constantly yelling "Let me back in, coach!" Dave went on to become a star player at Boise Jr. College and at the University of Oregon and then as a Football Hall of Fame player with the San Francisco 49ers. I took care of other members of his family, some of whom also played for professional teams for short times.

One brother was Joe. I took care of Joe for many years until I retired from active practice. Joe had the misfortune of having a pituitary tumor when he was about twelve years old. When the tumor was removed he lost his vision (a known complication of this type of surgery as the optic chiasm resides right next to the pituitary.) Because Joe had some vision before the surgery he was in the habit of doing things he had always done before. I was constantly patching him up because he had run his motorcycle or bicycle into a pole or fencepost on the farm - he would misjudge by a few feet from where he remembered the object to be. He walked all over Vale and Ontario using a white cane to probe for obstructions but he still managed to walk into poles and would come in periodically for stitches. He would memorize the number of steps it took from a curb to where he would turn into a house and was usually quite accurate. Because of his legitimate disability he received help from the state after his parents died. Also because his pituitary had been removed, he needed complete hormone support and this became somewhat of a problem. Thyroid and cortisone supplements he could take by mouth, but testosterone had to be given by injection or by implants. After we had been giving him injections for years the state went on an economy kick and stopped authorizing the testosterone. When I appealed the denial I was informed that the only reason they would authorize testosterone was for sexual dysfunction. They didn't understand my explanation that this man had lost his pituitary gland and couldn't make testosterone on his own. I finally wrote back that Joe had tried a marriage that didn't last real long, and maybe he did have some sexual dysfunction --- and I emphasized that sexual dysfunction was not the reason for his need of hormones. We finally were able to give him the shots he needed. We had continued to provide them at our expense but the official arguments were made by non-medical people and these kinds of decisions by non-medical persons are continuing to drive practitioners up the proverbial wall. Another example of bureaucratic bumbling I encountered occurred while I was taking care of a lady with pernicious anemia. People with this diagnosis are deficient in vitamin B12, resulting in serious anemia and neurological problems. Without supplemental B12 (usually injections are necessary) the patients can die from the disease. I argued till I was blue in the face but the welfare officials stood by their decision that no treatment with vitamins was authorized. In desperation I finally re-submitted the application with the diagnosis of Pernicious Anemia and requesting the medication "cyancobalamine" (which is the chemical name for Vitamin B12) by injection and the request was finally authorized.

Speaking of football players, I had the pleasure of meeting Bill McColl when I was a Vale JC (member of the Junior Chamber of Commerce) and he was on a lecture tour. Bill was playing football for the Chicago Bears football team while he was going to medical school in Chicago. He was in a class ahead of me at the University of Chicago Medical School but his graduation was delayed because he couldn't go to school during the football season. He had worked out a program between the University of Chicago and Northwestern University near Chicago so that he could get his whole medical school finished in about five or six years while still playing football in season. Bill was one of the nicest people in the world – a true gentle giant – except to his opponents on the football field. He had been an all-American player at Stanford. After he completed medical school he went into the field of orthopedics and did some very fine charitable work doing reconstructive surgery on children in Korea for which he received lots of recognition, and about which he was lecturing to JCs around the country. I saw him once more, years later, at a medical meeting and he was barely able to walk because of his football knee injuries. At that time knee replacements were not highly successful but I'm sure he was able to get some relief within a few years.

As my practice increased I had to add more staff to keep up with the increased load. I added a nurse to help with the patients, and kept Carol more in the office/receptionist role. Ann Eubanks had been trained as a RN at the hospital in Baker City quite a few years previously when Baker had a nursing program. She was from local pioneer families of McElroy, Lawrence and Zimmershied. She and her husband "Toe" seemed to know everyone in the county. Ann worked for me for many years until she died of a rapidly progressive malignancy. Ann's niece, Ann Kindschy, worked in the office for awhile. Shirley Harrod, who was to become Carol's sister-in-law, worked part time. Theron Richardson, who was secretary of both local irrigation districts worked at the irrigation district office next door to my office. He had done some accounting work while in the military service and he started helping us with our billing and accounting chores. He continued to help us when he moved to Ontario to work in a CPA office, and then later when I moved the office to Ontario, he joined us as a full-time office manager for many years. Another part-time employee we had for a time was Jessie Monson. Jessie was a very efficient and attractive mother of two boys and a girl. She helped with some of the billing and accounting chores. She had a string of horribly bad luck which exemplifies the expression about bad things happening to good people. Her oldest son was tragically killed in an automobile accident; then, when she still had fairly young children in school, she unexpectedly died. I had seen her children on occasion but she had been going to a doctor in another town so I was not aware of any medical problem. I gradually learned over time that she had been seeing a "diet doctor" and was taking a lot of pills. It was about that time that some noted pathologists were starting to understand a rash of unexpected deaths all over the country – mostly occurring in relatively young women. It was finally determined that many of these women had been taking a combination of appetite suppressant pills and this regimen was known as the "Rainbow Pill" program. Medications included in the variety of pills given in this program were amphetamines, diuretics, digitalis, and thyroid. The rationale for this combination of drugs apparently was to use the amphetamines (like the speed and "meth" currently being so abused) to jazz people up to burn more calories in addition to decreasing their appetite; the diuretics were to make them lose weight by dumping water; the digitalis was used because at high (actually toxic) levels it induced mild nausea and thereby decreased the appetite; and the thyroid was to increase their metabolism to burn more calories. As the pathologists were beginning to get a handle on this diet regime they found that the diuretics were causing potassium deficiencies which made the heart more prone to arrhythmias, the digitalis also had adverse cardiac effects at high doses, and the amphetamines and thyroid made the heart more irritable – the result being sudden cardiac death from arrhythmias. As this knowledge became more publicized these diet programs lost favor, but during the time they were popular far too many innocent lives were lost. I never knew if this was why Jessie died but I have had this suspicion for many years. It was a sad misuse of medications. For those who have never practiced medicine you would be amazed at how much pressure patients can put on a physician to get medicines that might later turn out to be harmful.

In Vale I had my first introduction to hunting. I had been brought up in a gentle non-hunting family. I was the only member of my family that ever had a gun, first a BB gun, and then a single shot 22 rifle, with which I earned some sharpshooter medals at Boy Scout camp. In Vale

90

I learned that almost everyone went hunting and fishing. It was so much a part of the culture that I found that even my pregnant patients would accept my absence at their delivery - if I was hunting. Their husbands had always made a big thing of hunting so to their way of thinking it was an important annual event. They did not take kindly however to my being away for a family vacation or to take a continuing education course. Theron was a big help in getting me started in hunting, and he did a lot over many years to train my boys in proper and safe hunting techniques. One day we had both Theron's family and my family out in the hills doing some target practice and "plinking" and I found out how overconfident patients can be about their doctor's abilities. Somehow one of the guns went off accidentally and the adults were immediately concerned and were greatly relieved that no one was hurt. Teresa, Theron's youngest daughter, sensed the parents' alarm and said "It's OK – Dr. Daniels is here" implying that I could take care of any emergency. There are a lot of things that happen that are beyond a doctors ability to fix. I enjoyed the hiking and the scenery, and did do some hunting. Over the years I got a couple of deer, and one elk, and a variety of birds. Hunting to me was most important as an acceptable means to get out into the wild and get a break from the office. One time when I was deer hunting on a warm day I stretched out in the sun to rest. I was extremely tired at the time and fell asleep. When I woke up I was surprised to find two of the cutest little coyote pups sniffing my feet. I'm glad it wasn't a bear or other unfriendly critter. Another time, while archery hunting, I came across a group of does and fawns who didn't seem to be aware of my presence. I spent about an hour observing the dynamics of the herd and was fascinated to observe the "boss lady" apparently giving orders to the others. They seemed to have a functioning communication system and it was a great learning experience for me to watch the guard member of the group look intently and rotate her ears like a radar antenna while the others were dining.

The whole family, which consisted of myself, my wife Toddy, Don (b. 1952), Alan (b. 1953), Kathy (b. 1956), and De Wilda (b. 1959), enjoyed hiking and camping. We bought an old, pretty much worn out school bus (we couldn't afford anything more expensive at the time) and had fun converting it into a recreation vehicle. On a few occasions I drove the bus to the hospital when I was caring for someone in labor and was able to do some modification work on the bus while still being close to the patient. The children were small so we could build small beds for them and a bigger bed for Toddy and me. We took that bus on many weekend trips around Eastern Oregon and found some really neat

camping places and saw some beautiful scenery. In one episode we almost had a disaster. We were on a small back road near Sumpter and crossed a small creek, only to get high centered. It was late in the day so we decided to camp where we were and get help in the morning. We had a charcoal burner, and no other source of heat. We

De Wilda 3 Months Old - Vale, Oregon 1959

thought we had plenty of ventilation but had misjudged and woke up with headaches and weakness. De Wilda, the smallest, was the hardest

hit and showed more evidence of carbon monoxide poisoning than the rest of us. We managed to get some help and spent most of the day recovering at the house of some friends in Sumpter. Several men came to help us dig out from our high centered dilemma. We never used charcoal inside the bus again.

Camping in the Converted School Bus

Once in awhile somebody comes into your life that is special. This happened to me one cold, unpleasant evening in Vale. Two radio announcers from KSRV, an Ontario radio station, had been covering a Vale High School athletic event and I got word to them that they would be welcome at my house after the game for a hot cup of coffee or chocolate and a chance to warm up before heading home to Ontario. I knew that both were friends of my surgeon friend Gus Tanaka and I knew that they were good announcers but not much more. When they arrived at the house it was immediately apparent that both of these men were outstanding individuals and Toddy and I were immediately comfortable with them. We had a pleasant visit that evening and it was the beginning of a lifelong special friendship with Clint Bellows. Clint had a variety of jobs – from radio announcer to TV announcer in Boise to chemical product salesman to financial advisor with the Edward Jones investment brokerage company. He moved several times but while he lived in the Ontario area his family and ours spent many a camping trip together over many years. Whenever we got together, even after many months, it seemed like we would just pick up where we left off the last time. Clint had a wonderful singing voice and took the lead position in many musical productions. He served as mayor of Ontario before moving out of the area. He finished out his career as a trouble shooter for the Edward Jones Company going all over the country to help out wherever he was needed. We still manage to get together every year or two, either in New Mexico where he presently lives or in Ontario when he travels to visit friends and relatives. A few years ago he helped me scatter Toddy's ashes at one of our favorite camping spots that we shared many times.

When I started practice the welfare system was handled locally and with county funds. The decision as to who got help for medical conditions was in the hands of a single local manager. One weekend I saw an elderly lady with severe abdominal pain and admitted her to the hospital. I was able to make a diagnosis of a bowel obstruction and obtained a surgical consultation. We were unable to locate the welfare manager but because the situation required emergency intervention we proceeded to do the necessary surgery. The patient recovered nicely but the welfare manager refused to pay for the surgery because we hadn't obtained prior approval. I had to drive to Ontario, taking time out of my office practice, to plead the case. In spite of the fact that the patient had been getting welfare assistance and that we had tried to locate the proper person before surgery, the welfare official was adamant that we shouldn't have done the surgery without getting her approval first. I tried to explain to her that delaying surgery could result in a disaster (the old surgical adage is that you never let the sun rise or set on a bowel obstruction). She finally relented and agreed to pay the surgeon and the hospital some small amount and allowed me something like $20 dollars for assisting at surgery, making the diagnosis, and spending all of a weekend night with the patient. She advised me that this was to be a one time act on her part and that I should never let it happen again. I tried to explain that patients don't get sick only during working hours etc., and I assured her I would try very hard to keep it from happening again: "May I please have your phone number?"

"What for?"

"So I can call you at home to get your approval when we have
another emergency surgery!"

"You can't do that!"

"Yes I can!"

That was my first personal experience with non-medical officials dictating what a doctor can and can't do. There would be many more.

Before I really had any serious thought of moving to Ontario I ran for the Vale school board. I had been brought up in an academic atmosphere and I felt that Vale was placing far too much emphasis on sports. My goal was to try to change the emphasis more toward academic pursuits. I was severely trounced, which was probably a good thing because I decided to move to Ontario before my term would have been up if I had been elected.

When my practice was steady enough that we could start making plans for new projects I starting thinking of learning to fly. I had started a few lessons while in college but could not continue because of finances. Several people in town also wanted to have a plane available to use or to use for training, so we formed a flying club with somewhere around 12 to 15 members. We jointly bought a Piper Super Cub airplane and I was able to restart my effort to become a private pilot.

Grandpa Harvey Meyer Visits Vale c. 1961

94

Flying

When I was small there were very few airplanes. The year I was born was the year that Charles Lindbergh flew solo across the Atlantic Ocean in a single engine airplane. I think I saw a few early "barnstorming shows" and was always intrigued with the thought of flying. I was never particularly interested in the loops and rolls and spins that seemed to excite crowds but I always wanted to fly like the birds. Early in WWII there were many training programs all over the country to train pilots for the war. I recall seeing many training biplanes practicing not far from our house in Madison. While I was in college at Oberlin, Ohio in 1946 I couldn't resist taking a few flying lessons from Hap Harper who had obtained a brand new post-war Cessna 120 which was a side-by-side, two place airplane and had an 85 hp continental engine. I was able to get almost six hours of instruction before I totally ran out of money and couldn't fly again till I was in practice in Vale fourteen years later. There were several of us in Vale that wanted to fly but couldn't afford a plane of our own but were able to share expenses, so we formed a flying club. We looked at several planes before deciding on a Piper Super Cub which was a good compromise for the needs of the group. I think there were about 12 to 15 members with a wide variety of backgrounds and flying experience. Some had been military pilots in WWII, others were already using planes in their businesses, and at least one already had a plane of his own but wanted to have access to the Super Cub for ranch work.

Dorin in Supercub and Toddy Outside

Some of us were just starting to work on our licenses. After we got the Super Cub I started seriously to work on getting my private pilot license. By flying an hour or so at a time, whenever I could, I was able to get my certificate in about 3 months. A month and a half after I got my Private Pilot Certificate, Toddy, and I joined Dr. Thomas and his wife from Condon, Oregon on a trip to the national AAGP (American Academy of General Practice – which later evolved into the American Academy of Family Physicians) meetings in Miami, Florida. We flew in his Beech Bonanza and it was a great learning experience for me because he was a very experienced pilot and I was able to learn a lot about cross country flying. At that meeting there were several members of the Flying Physicians Association present so we declared an impromptu meeting to be held in the Bahamas. Whoever arranged that trip did a masterful job of planning by starting the slower planes out first and the faster planes later so as to arrive about the same time. He even arranged for the Coast Guard to run escort for our dozen or so planes while flying over the water. The unforeseen problem with his precise scheduling was that his calculations were so good that we all arrived at the Bahamas within a few minutes of each other and the sleepy-sounding, slow-talking British tower operator was completely overwhelmed and flustered. It was an enjoyable side trip.

Dr & Mrs Thomas, Toddy & Dorin, Beach Bonanza - Bahamas 1961

After I had my license I was able to use the Super Cub in my business for going to meetings and an occasional house call. Because the Super Cub was a two-place airplane it wasn't big enough to take my family on trips, and because there were so many co-owners it was sometimes difficult to get the plane when wanted. Dr. Jim Mann who was practicing in Parma, Idaho and Tom Gray, a veterinarian in Vale, had young children and also wanted to have access to a family-friendly plane, so the three of us went together and got a Stinson Station Wagon which was an older (1946, I think) four-place airplane that we could use for family trips. The Stinson was slow but stable and was a very comfortable plane to fly. For quite awhile I kept access to both planes because they each had strong advantages for certain circumstances. My greatest use of airplanes over the years was to save travel time going to meetings and for family vacations. I also used the planes for distributing materials for mass polio immunization programs and for flying to small towns to give training to emergency personnel. I also made a few house calls which tested my newly-obtained flying skills. Not long after I got my license I made a call in the Super Cub to a rancher outside of Harper. He had a fast four-place Piper Comanche airplane and a very small air strip. He would typically use the highway for takeoff and landing and often taxied up a fairly steep driveway to park in his front yard. I didn't know his "highway"

96

habits and, as I was flying the Super Cub I thought the gravel strip would be simple. I made a good landing, although with white knuckles as I had never landed on that short a strip before. I made the house call and found a very sick man but decided that he probably had Colorado Tick Fever (not Rocky Mountain Spotted Fever) and let him stay home to suffer in private. I drew some blood for lab tests so he wouldn't have to go to the lab. He did recover.

Another flying house call I made defied so many odds that a Hollywood screen writer wouldn't write a script from it because it was so unlikely that no one would believe the story. Early one summer morning I got a call from a patient, Jasper Perry, who lived next to the Malheur River along Highway 20 between Harper and Juntura. Jasper had the only phone in the whole area. He didn't give a lot of detail but insisted that I come up to the scene of a highway accident several miles west of his house. He had promised the victims that he would get a doctor to come. He admitted that the ambulance had already been called from Ontario but as the highway was undergoing major reconstruction and was at the small boulder stage it was known that the ambulance would be very slow. Highway 20 is one of the three major East-West highways crossing Oregon and there are no good detours for this area so driving that summer was very slow and tedious. The road was, and still is, a two lane road so there was no way to block one lane while using the other lane. I argued that there was not much I could do at the scene and suggested that I meet the victims at the hospital but Jasper insisted that I come so I finally agreed. I decided to use the Super Cub, instead of driving, because of the bad roads and went to the airport to see if the plane was available. It was in the hanger and no one had signed up to use it that morning so I rolled it out and headed up the canyon. After I passed Harper at about 500 feet I started looking for the car wreck. I finally spotted the wreck approximately twelve miles west of Harper and noted that there were a few cars at the scene and was glad that someone was staying with the victims till help arrived. The accident scene was in a fairly narrow part of the canyon and there was no place to land there so I circled and headed further west looking for a place to land. I had never made an off airport landing but I had the perfect plane for the purpose. I finally found a fairly small hay field along the edge of the river which appeared to have been recently cut and didn't appear to have been recently irrigated so I put the plane down with a good landing just as though I had done it before. I climbed out of the plane, grabbed my medical bag and climbed up a bank to the road just as a minister and his family from Ohio were driving by from the direction of the accident. I flagged them and told them I was a doctor and asked if they would take me back to the accident scene. They were happy to oblige and seemed to think it was real cool to be part of the scenario of a doctor dropping out of the sky to help at an accident scene in the middle of nowhere.

When I arrived at the scene I quickly learned that the couple in the wrecked Volkswagen Bug had been driving all night, much of the time on very difficult roads, and the husband who was driving went off of the road hitting a bank and disabling the car. I also learned that he was diabetic and on insulin, and it was apparent that the wife was shaken up and had minor bruises but she was extremely concerned about her husband who was rather incoherent. His status was one of those situations where clinically he had suffered a concussion but it was impossible to know how much of the problem was actually due to diabetes out of control. The fact that I looked to be about 20 to 25 years old, even though I was in my mid thirties, didn't console this distressed woman. At that time there was no way to check blood sugars in the field so all I could do was to check him for neurological changes while waiting for the ambulance to take him to the hospital. After I had checked him enough that I didn't think he was in mortal danger I tried to console the distraught wife and just talked to her to try to give her some reassurance. After visiting awhile I realized that her perspective of the situation was that she had an injured diabetic husband and they were not in the middle of nowhere – they were beyond the end of nowhere – and were being tended to by a stranger who seemed too young to be a doctor. As I visited some more the conversation went something like this: "Where are you from?" - "Chicago." - "Oh, that's where I went to medical school." At this point she relaxed a bit as she began to realize that I was at least familiar with civilization. She asked me what medical school I had attended to which I responded "The University of Chicago" and she relaxed some more. We visited some more and she said that her husband's diabetes doctor was Dr Kenyon at the University of Chicago to which I responded "I know Dr. Kenyon - he was the endocrinology professor who taught me how to treat diabetes." My status rapidly changed from an unknown country hick to as close to a godlike creature who dropped out of the sky as I have ever been. When the ambulance finally arrived I helped load the patient and the much relieved wife into the ambulance and had another passerby take me back to the airplane. I had made my first landing in a hayfield, and was now about to make my first hayfield takeoff. I treated the husband in the hospital for a few days while he recovered from his concussion and got his diabetes stabilized. Of all the hundreds of thousands of people in Chicago it is a wild coincidence that I knew the patient's doctor. It makes you wonder: was it "Coincidence" - or something more?

My involvement with aviation continued in many forms. I became a Pilot Medical Examiner and went to several fairly lengthy training sessions. I gave flight physicals to quite a few airline pilots who lived in the area and commuted to San Francisco or Chicago or Denver for their jobs. I also was appointed by the FAA to be a crash investigator to assist local law enforcement personnel with airplane crash investigations. Unfortunately there were several local area crashes, some of which resulted from incredibly stupid pilot behavior. I will spare the reader the gruesome details of these events.

As I look back on some of our family trips I wonder how we ever managed to take vacation trips to Tennessee and Wisconsin in the Stinson. We had put some jump seats in the luggage compartment for the smallest children and traveled with very little luggage, but to fly that far in a four-place plane into which we had stuffed a family of six, and only went about one hundred miles an hour, we were either very courageous or very stupid. (Maybe both.) As the children got larger we gradually got bigger planes. In spite of the crowded space and its slow speed the Stinson was the only plane we had over the years in

Family Trip in Stinson 1962 - Alan, Toddy, Don, Kathy, Dorin & DeWilda

which my wife was even close to comfortable. She really didn't like to fly.

The most fun medical meetings I attended were the annual Flying Physicians Association meetings. At most medical meetings everyone talks medicine but at these meetings everyone talks airplanes. Many lectures and demonstrations of aviation-related procedures and activities were both entertaining and instructional. One time at a Reno meeting we went to Stead Air Force base and were given instruction in survival techniques. The instructors were great and we learned about eating bugs and worms, how to crash a small plane in the mountains and survive, and some tips about keeping your cool in the midst of total chaos and terror. These instructors told us that for survival purposes the best weapon is a 22 caliber pistol, because you can carry a lot of ammunition and you won't ruin much meat. When asked by one cynic if a .22 pistol would really provide much protection against a bear, the instructor said "no problem – just shoot it in the eye!" He meant what he said but I think most of us non-military types would have had a hard time being that accurate, especially when scared stiff. I think those military survival experts have their own little niche of "crazy" but I would sure like to have one of them with me if I was ever lost in the wilderness.

Which planes did I like best? For pure fun and the ability to land in difficult situations I'll take the Super Cub. My wife never liked the kite-like feeling she experienced in that plane. For getting somewhere fast and comfortably I'll go with the Cessna 210 which went about 200 miles per hour and could carry 6 people.

I continued to fly for many years and became partners with a group of Ontario businessmen and we shared bigger and faster planes. I finally had to quit flying because of diabetes after more than 900 hours of flying, and had some flying time in about twelve different models of aircraft. I never tried to learn to fly twin engine planes but I did study for and obtained an instrument flight certification so that I could fly to meetings in less than perfect weather conditions. The picture below was taken a year or two after the St. Helens eruption.

Mt. St Helens - Picture From Plane I Was Flying

Volunteering

Volunteerism, public service, and teaching all seemed to merge into my life after I started my medical practice in 1958 in Vale, a small town in eastern Oregon's Malheur County, an area which is bigger than New Hampshire and has a population of about 30,000 or three persons per square mile. Ontario is the largest center of population in this north eastern part of the county and is about 18 miles east of Vale.

If there was any one incident that started my long-term dedication to volunteering, it was a call I got one evening from the state police who asked me to go to the scene of an automobile accident on Vines Hill which was several miles west of Vale. In those days, the state police radios could only reach their offices from a limited number of locations. They were able to communicate from the Vale side of Vines Hill, and because I was the closest physician, I was asked to go to the scene because I could get there faster than the ambulance from Ontario.

Perhaps some background about emergency services and accident investigation procedures in our state in the late 1950s would be helpful. Accident fatalities, homicides, suicides, and any suspicious deaths were to be examined by the coroner - which at that time was a political position with no specific qualifications or requirements. A policy at the time, of which I was not aware, seemed to indicate that in the case of a traumatic or suspicious death, the body was not to be touched until examined by the coroner. The coroner in our area was also the main undertaker in the county, and he resided in Ontario.

The road was wet from rain as I arrived at the accident scene. A state police officer had witnessed the car in question go off the road and roll over. By the time I arrived, a half hour or so after the accident, the policeman was standing by, waiting for me and for the ambulance. The car had held two prominent Ontario businessmen, both of whom had been thrown out as the car rolled. One was semi-conscious and was obviously suffering from a head injury. The other appeared lifeless and was lying face down in a half-inch deep mud puddle. This was before seat belts were common – they might have saved both men from death and damage.

Not long after I arrived, the ambulance (which was also the hearse,) arrived and the coroner/driver/ambulance attendant – all the same person! – declared that one had died of accidental causes and put both the living and the dead into the hearse/ambulance. They were taken to Ontario – one to the hospital and one to his mortuary. The policeman, following protocol, had not touched the body of the apparently dead person.

I was haunted from then on about a system that was so flawed that a policeman was not to do anything to help the injured, or supposedly dead, until the scene could be checked by an untrained political appointee, and that the ambulance/hearse was run by a person who I suspect did not even have basic first aid training, and also who had what I considered to be a major conflict of interest. I am haunted to this day by the thought that the person that died that evening might not have been killed outright, but could have just been knocked out and drowned in a half inch mud puddle. The fact that there was a police officer on the scene almost before the car stopped rolling, and that he did nothing to allow the patient to breath if he was alive, started me on a mission of trying to improve a failed system.

I was not alone in my endeavors. Efforts were already underway to replace the coroner system in Oregon with a medical examiner system where examinations of suspicious or unusual deaths would be done by trained medical personnel, usually an MD who took special forensic training before being qualified for the position. Also in the planning stages were the beginnings of what was to evolve into EMT training and certification at a national level. I did not wait for these programs to evolve, but started a local program of training for volunteers from the fire department and volunteer ambulance drivers.

I also tried to get law enforcement officers to ignore the "don't touch" principle and at least check for airway obstructions and bleeding – procedures that might allow a person to live – and not worry if that meant that the body had been touched. I strongly felt that the possibility of saving a life should take precedent over the possibility of altering an accident or crime scene that was going to be examined by someone who didn't really know what to look for anyhow.

I spent many an evening giving glorified first aid courses to enthusiastic fire and ambulance volunteers who were thirsty for knowledge, and who were dedicated to serving their fellow citizens. They were serving without pay and wanted to do the best they could. They were exposed to some very gruesome farm accident situations, as

102

well as more routine medical and traumatic circumstances, and served vast areas far from help, so I felt that giving them more than basic first aid training would be a real boost to the community. Most of these volunteers were of modest means, but they were so grateful that they chipped in and bought me a nice winter jacket to express their appreciation. Later, Treasure Valley Community College in Ontario started a program similar to what I had done in Vale. It became an area-wide program for all volunteer emergency personnel in the area as well as the evolving private ambulance services.

I spent many nights on that project in Ontario, giving comprehensive lectures and discussion sessions on a vast variety of emergency medical and traumatic situations. This had to be done twice for each subject so that the emergency personnel could split evenings and still keep the community covered. That meant three evening hours twice a week in addition to my already long hours as a physician. Frequently I didn't have time to eat before going to the classes. I finally reached a breaking point from sheer fatigue.

When I announced that I was going to have to cut back, and that they would have to find someone else to do the teaching I was met with rather unpleasant threats that I "couldn't do that." I found out as I probed a bit further, the main reasons they didn't want me to quit were that: (a) they couldn't find anyone else to teach for free; and (b) they were receiving matching money for my free service and were using that money for other projects. They never thought of offering me any remuneration for my services, but were upset when they found out that they were going to lose the matching funds if I quit.

Not long after I stopped my emergency medical teaching the EMT program evolved with national standards so that everyone would do the same thing in a standardized way. What was to be taught and how it was to be taught became protocol driven, and my style of teaching became a thing of the past. I had wanted the emergency persons to have a broad base of knowledge to which they could apply common sense. For many years I got expressions of appreciation from those early students as to how much they learned in my courses.

Many years after my experience with the training of local emergency personnel, while I was involved with the Certificate of Needs Committee, the committee's attorney adviser became ill at lunch. I was at the same table with him and saw him turn grey and slump in his chair. I immediately jumped up and guided him to the floor and he improved fairly quickly, but after a few minutes when we tried to help him sit up he immediately faded again. I had someone call 911 and a first response unit was there within minutes. They took his blood pressure and found it to be low. They tried to sit him up to recheck his blood pressure and his pressure dropped severely. He obviously had postural hypotension but the underlying cause was not clear and it was apparent that he needed hospital evaluation.

The ambulance arrived a few minutes later and the ambulance attendants started through the same protocol at which time I stopped them from sitting him up again. I told them that we had seen him get distressed not once, but twice, when trying to get into an upright position and that he should be transported to the hospital without further ado. I was told quite firmly that once they arrived on the scene they were in charge and that they were going to follow their protocol. I again insisted that he be transported without another upright blood pressure check. I was rather gruffly advised that even though I was a doctor they were going to do their prescribed routine and that I had no authority with them unless I assumed full responsibility and went with them in the ambulance. I had no choice but to go with them as I felt that if he had suffered a heart attack, another test of his intolerance to upright blood pressure testing might be catastrophic. On the way to the hospital his blood pressure dropped severely again and I was able to get some help for him by ordering some atropine which helped stabilize him.

Fortunately he recovered without problems and was back at work with us in a few days. I was extremely impressed with the advances in emergency care that had occurred in the intervening twenty five or so years, but as I thought back on my early volunteer teaching days when I had spent so much time training emergency personnel I still wished that protocol-driven responses had not become so rigid that common sense was not allowed to come in to play.

My volunteer and teaching activities expanded to state as well as local levels in the fields of health planning, and as a faculty member of the newly formed Department of Family Medicine at the Oregon Health Sciences University serving as a preceptor for medical students and family practice residents.

The Family Medicine Specialty
And My Small Role In Its Evolution

Prior to WWII a fairly high percentage of MDs went into the practice of medicine after a one year internship at a teaching hospital or a medical school. They usually had finished a four year premedical program prior to a four year medical school education. During WWII there was a great need for increased numbers of physicians, and medical schools helped meet the demand by intensified and accelerated programs that compressed the time frame for graduation.

After the war, many of these newly trained doctors, as well as many of the others who had been pressed into military service, returned to civilian life and set their sights on becoming "specialists." Also there were many servicemen who had been serving for several years, who had seen a lot of miscry and trauma, and who set their sights on getting an education and going into medical fields. The GI Bill allowed many who had not thought that they could get advanced educations to actually achieve their dreams of getting an education and bettering their lot in life. Returning GIs flooded the college campuses all over the country, and most were serious students, so competition for advanced training became intense. As these highly motivated students worked their way through college and applied for admission into the medical schools, the deans of admissions at the medical schools found themselves with a new challenge. They were flooded with huge overloads of applicants, many of whom were extremely well qualified. There was enough demand for medical school positions that the admissions offices could select from only straight A students, and subsequently pick their roster based on other criteria. This pretty much eliminated a fairly large group of desirable applicants who previously would have been considered.

It is my impression that this was a definite factor in the changing attitudes in American medicine. I feel that a lot of altruistic and compassionate candidates were eliminated in favor of the straight A students. Most of those chosen became excellent physicians, but some became brilliant blobs without any "people skills." Many of these highly accomplished students could have gone in any direction, but saw the chance for big money in the medical field, and were more money-oriented than their predecessors who tended to consider the practice of medicine as a calling, a service to their fellow man.

In the 1950s there was a definite trend toward specialization. Technology was exploding, and exciting advances made increased specialization a necessity, but the trend was also paralleled by an attitudinal change that the general, non-specialist doctor was becoming an inferior product. Older physicians who had held down the home front during the war were starting to retire and replacements were not easy to find, especially in the smaller towns. The medical schools, dominated by specialists, tended to imply that general practice physicians could not be good doctors, and the teachers encouraged their students to specialize.

From the time I was a small child I had been interested in becoming a doctor of the type that took care of me and our family. "The Family Doctor" took care of the entire family, made house calls, and was compassionate and dedicated. I never dreamed that these wonderful persons would someday be considered to be not as good as the newer specialists. When I finished medical school I still felt that my calling was to be a general practitioner in a small town and I bucked the "go specialist" trend. This declaration by me was a great disappointment to some of the officials at my medical school who felt that with my research training and family history I should go into academic medicine, teaching, or research, or if I really wanted to take care of patients I should consider some super specialty. While in internship in Portland, Oregon, at St Vincent Hospital, I witnessed some extremely capable general practitioners, and a variety of skill levels of a variety of specialists. I became further convinced that good medicine could be practiced by a generalist but I also realized that I would be a better doctor if I took a bit more training than the usual one year internship. Some of the very fine GPs encouraged me to apply for a Meade Johnson scholarship for extra training in general practice, which I did, and which I received for my residency training in 1957/58. There were only four of these awards given in the entire country that year so I felt greatly honored.

Throughout the country a realization was developing that there was still a role for the general physician, and that specialization for everyone was not a good answer to the health needs of the country, particularly in small towns. Some very good doctors around the country sparked a movement to upgrade the skills of the general practitioner, and to develop a certification program through which the GP could be certified as a specialist. This movement was spearheaded and supported by the American Academy of General Practice (AAGP) which had become the prime advocate of continuing education for general practitioners. This organization and its related state affiliates became well known for their requirements of continuing education as a condition of continuing membership. This became a large undertaking as there was a lot of resistance from the specialty groups who did not want their "superior" status diluted. In the early planning stages of this movement there were many local, state, and national meetings where there was an attempt to reach some consensus as to what should be taught and how the knowledge should be tested in order to qualify for board certification. Because I was one of the very few Meade Johnson scholarship award winners who had actually taken extra training in general practice, I was invited to participate in some of these planning sessions at both the state and national levels. Some of these meetings were very discouraging to me as I realized for the first time how severe the resistance was from many of the specialty groups.

One planning session that I attended at the University of Oregon Medical School was chaired by Dr. "Hod" Lewis who was noted as a superb physical diagnostician. I had not known him before but his reputation for diagnostic skills was legendary. In teaching physical diagnosis to the students he would expect them to take about an hour for each patient for the chest examination alone. This was great for teaching some of the nuances of difficult diagnostic techniques but it was a terribly impractical approach for the busy doctor with a waiting room full of patients. He disturbed me with a comment that he didn't think the idea of training for general practice would really work out because it was totally impossible for a doctor to be trying to take care of a patient with a broken leg in the emergency room, while following a patient on the medical floor who was in congestive heart failure, and at the same time following and delivering a patient in labor. His condescending attitude rubbed me the wrong way, and though I was still very shy in those days I did speak up and told him that I didn't know how he had come up with that particular combination of problems but that I had dealt with that same exact scenario two weeks before, plus trying to deal with an office full of patients at the same time! This man, in spite of his noted brilliance, had no clue as to the demands put on the small town doctor and he could not possibly have survived in a small town practice.

At a national meeting in Kansas City in 1962, sponsored by the AAGP, most of the attendees were high powered directors of medical education from major teaching hospitals around the nation, representatives from various specialty organizations, and a few of us from general practice. There were many lectures from the high powered persons giving their views on what they felt should be included in the curriculum for the new specialty. One particularly arrogant (and yes, he was obnoxious also,) surgeon gave his opinion that trainees for general practice should not be taught anything about surgery. His reasoning was that in his hospital a general practitioner was not allowed into the operating room even if he had referred the patient, and he was not allowed to assist with the operation. The next day I happened to be at his table for lunch and he had already had a few martinis and was commenting that it sure was funny "ha ha" that whenever an internist referred him a case of appendicitis it had usually already ruptured. Internists generally have had no surgical training and this surgeon did not seem to understand that with surgical training, the very training that he previously stated should not be taught, a doctor would have a better understanding of living pathology and would make better diagnoses even if he did not do the surgery.

It took many years but eventually the criteria for training and the testing procedures were worked out, and the specialty of Family Practice was born in 1969 as the 20th recognized Board specialty. The exam was quite comprehensive so that the specialists in other fields could not claim that our specialty status came too easily. I took the first examination, given in 1970, and was then Board certified as a specialist. To deflect possible complaints from other specialists, this new Board was set up so that the specialty status was not a lifetime grant. In order to maintain the specialty status it was required that recertification examinations be satisfactorily completed every six or seven years. I took recertifying examinations in 1976, 1982 and 1989 which allowed me to be certified until I retired from active practice in 1994. There continues to this day a lot of controversy as to what privileges a Family Practice Specialist should be allowed. Hospitals, insurance companies, and local medical politics all dictate their own criteria, but at least the family doctor now is better qualified, and has received more recognition than in the past.

Ontario

When I moved to Ontario I joined the Tanaka Clinic. I had learned enough about the medical community to know that I was in an unusually blessed environment. My medical colleagues were competent, concerned, and compassionate. I had learned that we had an unusually cooperative medical community and the atmosphere of cooperation between groups, individuals and the hospitals was outstanding. I had become aware of other communities where infighting, back-biting, and feuding made practice a chore instead of a joy, so I knew that this was where I wanted to stay. I had been in the area long enough that I knew that this was home. For many months Dr. Gus Tanaka had been talking to me, encouraging me to join his clinic group. We had a wonderful working relationship and I had great respect for his surgical skills and for his impeccable ethical standards. I also liked the business arrangement that he proposed which was basically that we would have independent practices and would share ancillary services such as lab and x-ray. This format appealed to both of us as our time and income would be tied to our own efforts and was not related to any other physician's productivity. This format was already in place with Dr. Flanagan, an internist, who left the Ontario Clinic and joined Gus and his father Ben when their clinic was built in 1958. When I made the decision to move to Ontario, Dr. Tanaka started building an addition to the clinic to accommodate my practice. I moved to Ontario a couple of months before my addition was completed because Dr. Ben had taken a trip to Japan and was going to be gone for quite awhile so I camped temporarily in his office.

When I arrived in Ontario I had several surprises. First, and not a great surprise, was the fact that a high percentage of my Vale patients followed me to Ontario. Second, and a bit more surprising, was the fact that some Vale residents who had not come to me while I was in Vale now started coming to see me in Ontario. Third, and most surprising of all, was the fact that some patients who had seen me in Vale and who conveniently forgot to pay for my services started coming to see me in Ontario and actually started paying for their care. I gathered from a few comments that the perception was that now that I was in a bigger town I must be a better doctor. I never quite understood that philosophy. My practice grew rapidly and my obstetrical patient load exploded. Living closer to the hospital dramatically improved my efficiency.

When we were preparing for the move and were looking for a house in Ontario we checked several available houses and nothing seemed quite right. We were starting to get a bit discouraged until a new listing showed up which we immediately checked. It was a farm at the west edge of town and the owner was getting old and farming was getting too hard for him. He was also having health problems. There were

Our 1st Ontario Home - DeWilda, Don, Kathy, and Pat the Dog

thirty five acres on the farm and he had rented it out to another farmer for the last few years. The house was a small two bedroom home with one bath, a kitchen, a small dining room, a nice but fairly small living room, a small laundry room, and a small part basement. All these smalls added up to a too-small house for our growing family. However, there was a barn on the property which we used to store all sorts of junk. The location was great – I could be at the hospital and office within about five minutes and we liked the idea of having space around us. We decided that we could live in cramped quarters for a while until we could build a new house on the property. My wife had always been interested in house design and drew up her own plans. The boys had to use double-decker beds in the laundry room for their

bedroom, and the one bathroom was a bit of a problem with two boys and two girls plus the two adults. It seemed that the longer we were in the tiny house the bigger the proposed new house plans got. We continued to rent out the farm to the row crop farmer who had been

Our Second Ontario House - Built in 1965 - Pictured 40 Years Later

farming it for a few years before we arrived. After several years the farmer was having trouble getting irrigation water on schedule – we were at the end of the ditch and delivery was not always reliable enough for row crops so he stopped renting our land. When he stopped farming Alan, our number two son, was in high school and he took over the farm operation and put the land into alfalfa hay. He borrowed some equipment at first and we got an old tractor to do some of the work. We had to contract for the cutting and baling. When it came to picking up the bales of hay Alan got some of his friends to help load and stack the hay the old fashioned way – by hand. That is brutal work but he was able to make some spending money.

Most of my time was spent taking care of patients. My office practice became very large and I was never able to keep on a tight schedule. I always felt it was more important to take care of a patient's problem at the time rather than limit my time with them. My poor office staff was constantly trying to juggle patients to meet my impossible schedule. I did a lot of surgical assisting, mostly on my own patients but I was also frequently asked to help on other doctors' patients. As my obstetrical load increased I was spending more time at the hospital and it got to be pretty much of a routine to put in fourteen to sixteen hour days. There were steadily increasing demands from the hospital to participate in expanding committee functions involving the paper work being mandated from insurance companies and governmental agencies. Many of our committee meetings were scheduled for seven a.m. so as not to conflict with office hours. Some of the meetings were in the evening.

After Dr. Ben Tanaka retired we were very fortunate to get Dr. Andrew Peterson to join us in the clinic. Andy was an internal medicine specialist who had taken extra training in pulmonary medicine. He was a great addition to our clinic and to the community. Even now, he is keeping most of us retired folks tuned up and many of us are fearful of his eventual retirement. Like many older folks I don't want to have to look for a new doctor. Dr. Mann had come after I did and was well established. Another doctor that joined our clinic for several years was Ken Pfaff. Ken had been orphaned at a fairly young age and had spent some time in an orphanage. He went to work while quite young and was a professional boxer for awhile. He joined the paratroopers in WWII (probably underage) and I think he had some combat experience. He worked his way through college and then taught school for awhile before going to medical school. A small addition was built on to the clinic to make room for him. He was a good doctor but his practice dwindled after a few years because he

111

became more and more fixated on the politics of land use planning. He couldn't seem to understand that patients came to see him for medical problems and not to discuss state politics. He was rather bitter when he moved on.

For many years we had no emergency room coverage and a small number of us covered on a rotating basis. For quite awhile almost all of the doctors took turns to spread the load but that system broke down when we got some new specialists in town who didn't want to cover the emergency room and treat patients outside of their own specialty field. We gradually got down to about eight or ten of the general practitioners, pediatricians, surgeons and OB/GYN specialists who would cover the ER. We all continued to be on call at all times for our own patients if we were in town. About the same time there were some changing attitudes in the general population. Patients were beginning to utilize emergency rooms at hospitals for more and more problems that previously would have been treated in the doctors' offices. The result of these changes was that the evening and night calls at the emergency room were becoming very demanding and it was not unusual to be called to the emergency room many times throughout the night. In my case, having a busy general practice, I would frequently get called to the hospital to see my own patients in the ER on nights when I was not on call. The call rotation was designed to cover only those patients who had no established physician. We reached a point that several doctors were starting to make noises about leaving the community because the load was becoming so overwhelming. The hospital administrator at that time, Chuck Smith, realizing that the physicians were becoming so burned out that mass rebellion was imminent, started searching for ways to get some relief. It was finally decided to contract with one of the early ER physician organizations that had been started in the San Francisco Bay area by Dr. Mangold. Once the ER contract physicians were in place the local doctors were able to get some sleep at night and were able to assume a more normal home life. The ER coverage became a 24 hour service and the facility was dramatically improved. Our practices changed in the process because previously we had to interrupt our office practice to care for emergencies at the hospital and we could now stay on a bit more of a schedule.

We always tried to keep working conditions as close to fun as possible to avoid stagnation and burn out. After working through the night and coming to the office with no sleep it wasn't always easy to stay upbeat. My office staff had a very difficult time trying to accommodate my erratic schedule and they did as good a job of pacifying patients in the waiting room as could be expected. A patient was overheard in the waiting room one day after waiting well past her appointment time, saying to another patient "I sure hate waiting so long for the doctor but it's sure worth it because when I get back in the examining room I feel like I am the only patient that he has." I considered that comment to be a real compliment.

One of my long time nurses, Patsy Looney, had a great sense of humor and a very mischievous trait which was totally unpredictable. She and her husband lived in a house across the street and a few hundred feet towards town from our house so when I went to the hospital at night my car, or motorcycle, lights would swing across their bedroom window as I came out of my driveway. That is the background for an incident that left me sputtering and trying to explain things. I was in the middle of an exam on a lady I did not know well when Patsy casually asked if I had gone to the hospital for a delivery during the night. My answer was "Yes, Mrs. X had a baby boy." Her immediate and deadpan response was "I just wondered, I thought I heard you leave." I had to explain to the patient that our houses were close to each other etc. Another evening we had clothes in our dryer when the dryer quit working. Rather than leave wet clothes overnight my wife and I called Pat and explained our dilemma. We were promptly invited over and had a great visit while the clothes were in her dryer. The next day in a situation similar to the above incident she casually said "Oh, by the way – you left one of your socks at my house last night." Of course she didn't explain the circumstances so I was compelled to sputter out an explanation. Another time after returning from lunch I was examining a lady. I was using a powered exam table so I could raise the patient like a car on a grease rack using a foot pedal. I did it all the time: it saved me some stooping and the patients were used to it. When the patient was part way up on her ride towards the ceiling I heard her loudly say "What is that?" "What is what?" I replied. She was pointing to something on the ceiling that she was approaching as the table was rising. There between two rows of fluorescent lights directly over her head was a magazine centerfold type picture. No one took credit for that prank but Patsy was working that day. I had the picture removed – I thought one patient was enough for that situation.

Patsy wasn't the only one who kept things lively. One day I was getting ready to do a minor surgical procedure on a man. Some men were uncomfortable having a female nurse helping on this procedure so Theron, my business manager, would usually help. On this day the patient was a friend of Theron's and we were also introducing a medical student to office surgery. Long story short – as I was prepping the patient and the student was watching, Theron came through the door with a tray of instruments. The only problem was that instead of the usual scalpel, syringes, forceps, sutures, etc. the tray held a large rubber mallet (anesthesia), a vice-grip pliers, and tin snips. The student was the first to see the tray and his eyes got bigger and bigger. The patient was next to see the tray and he just about jumped off of the table. I was the last to see it as my back was towards to door. I realized that Theron was having fun with both his friend and the student. We had a good laugh, got the right tools, and proceeded with the operation. I often wondered what that student had to say when he got back to Portland and was telling his friends about the crazy doctor he was working with in Ontario.

My friends on the hospital staff also were not above a little practical joke activity. One time I was having bilateral hernias repaired by Dr. Tanaka. When I woke up after anesthesia and was in that fuzzy almost awake state I noticed that almost the whole surgery crew was hovering around my recovery room bed. Then I noticed that there were guppies swimming around in my IV bottle. About that time Dr. Tanaka came in to check on me and he had not been aware of the joke and he jerked the IV out of my arm because it looked so real. He had not been in on the prank and didn't realize how much work the crew had to go through to get that one set up. We all had a good laugh and I wondered why the crew was still hanging around until Dorothy, the head surgical nurse, put a very serious look on her face and told me that I had best check my incisions. Of course I was almost in panic mode as I hoped that nothing had gone wrong with the surgery. I immediately pulled the sheets down to check and there on each groin incision were nice big golden Christmas bows. Then I knew why the crew was staying around and was wondering if there was more to come. Fortunately there were no further pranks so I dozed a bit.

Sometimes humor comes from unexpected sources. Sometime in the mid 1960s a grade school classmate who had become a psychiatrist practicing in New Haven, Connecticut decided to move to the Seattle,

Washington area. I had not seen him for many years but he contacted my folks to find out where I lived and arrived at my office on a busy afternoon and sat in my office as I was trying to finish seeing patients so we could have some visiting time. After watching me pop into the office about six times to dictate chart notes he looked at me and with slow deliberative speech, his fingers tapping on the arm of his chair, he said, "Dorin, I sure would like to help you see patients so we could get out sooner but I've forgotten which end of the stethoscope to put in my mouth." That comment cracked me up. The next day we took Ed with the family to visit the Jordon Craters. Those craters have fresh looking lava flows, a volcanic crater, lava tubes, and some igloo shaped spatter cones. The impressive thing about the craters is how fresh the flow looks. Ed found a few pieces of scrap paper and some dry grass and quietly started a fire in one of he spatter cones and when the smoke was starting to show he yelled, "It's starting to blow!" Toddy had always been afraid of fire and De Wilda was on crutches at the time, so their efforts to run away were almost comical – in a grim sort of way. Neither Toddy nor De Wilda really thought the prank was funny.

As I have said elsewhere, I tried to arrange for something unusual or recreational for at least one day when I had students staying with me. I had been getting bugged repeatedly by a local insurance agent who wanted me to fly down to a ranch near Jordan Valley to do an insurance physical on a rancher who didn't ever seem to have time to come to town. For months I had been refusing his request because to be out of the office at least a half a day to do the job was totally unrealistic for the amount I was to be paid. When I heard that I was to get a student and his wife in a couple of weeks I called the agent and said that I might reconsider his request if he would pay the gas and find out where I was expected to land. Jordon Valley did not have an airstrip at that time. The agent was ecstatic as he really wanted to nail down that account. He was a pilot and he flew down to the ranch and checked out the neighbor's air strip and made all of the arrangements. A few days into the new student's rotation I told the student and his wife that we were going to be making a house call that they might enjoy, unless they were afraid of airplanes. This student and his wife were having some troubles resolving their goals. He was interested in practicing in a small town and she was more inclined to live in a big city. I knew that I wouldn't resolve their differences but I did want them to get an unusual experience. On the appointed day we got into the plane. At that time the plane I shared was a Cessna 206 which was a workhorse type plane that held 6 people. My oldest son Don was in an aviation training school and I believe he already had his commercial license; he flew the co-pilot position. In the middle seats were the student and his wife and in the back row was the insurance agent. The plane was fairly heavily loaded so we hoped the strip we were headed for was not real short. The insurance man had given us good directions and we found the strip without difficulty after a sight seeing trip over the Jordon Craters (a rather dramatic lava flow and small volcanic crater that looks like it just happened but is probably about 500 years old). We circled the air strip to look it over and landed without difficulty. Once we landed we were wondering where to park the plane. The owner of the airstrip drove to our plane within minutes of our landing and as we were visiting with him he stated that his plane was in the shop for its annual inspection, and that no one else ever used the strip so he suggested we just leave the airplane where it was in the middle of the runway. He had known that we were coming and was to take me to the neighbor's house where I would do the insurance physical. He was also going to loan a vehicle to the others in the plane so that they could tour the area and look at the grave site of Jean-Baptiste Charbonneau, Sacagawea's son, who was the baby on the Lewis and Clark expedition. Sacagawea's baby had been brought up and educated by Captain Clark, and had spent time in royal courts in Europe before returning to the American west as a guide, prospector, and mountain man. He had been traveling from California in 1866 and headed for the gold fields in Idaho and Montana when he contracted pneumonia and died near what is now Danner, Oregon, which was only a very short distance from Skinner Ranch where we landed.

As we were starting to go our own ways we heard a plane flying fairly high and the engine did not sound healthy. As we were watching, the distressed plane made a sudden turn and headed for the airstrip that we were parked on. We all immediately pushed our plane off of the landing strip so the plane whose engine was sounding worse and worse could have an unobstructed runway. We watched as the distressed plane came in high and made the highest bounce I have ever seen on a landing, but he finally made it down safely. The pilot of that plane said he was sure glad he had seen our plane on the runway because he was sure he wouldn't have recognized the airstrip as a place to land otherwise. Now there were two planes on the strip where "no one ever lands." A few minutes later a third plane landed – it was the partner of a two plane flight of friends who were flying from Boise, Idaho to

Reno, Nevada. Now there were three planes on the "never used" strip. Everyone seemed safe so we left for our planned pursuits and about an hour later I was driven back to the airstrip and there were now four planes on the field. The newest plane had brought in a mechanic. So much for the claim that the strip was never used by anyone but the owner! I have never left a plane on a runway since. My student and his wife saw the Charbonneau gravesite and some old ranches, and they had indeed had an unusual experience. For some other students we took them skiing, hiking, exploring, camping, or fishing depending on the season and their interests.

Medical Student at Charbonneau Grave

I got into computers fairly early as they were starting to come into the small business and medical offices. The first machine that I bought for office use was a Radio Shack TRS-80 Model II Micro Computer. The promotional literature states – *"The TRS-80 Model II microcomputer system, designed and manufactured by Radio Shack in Fort Worth, TX, was not intended to replace or obsolete the Model I. It was designed to take up where the Model I left off – a machine with increased capacity and speed in every respect, targeted directly at the small-business application market. The Model II contains a single-sided full-height Shugart 8-inch floppy drive, which holds 500k bytes of data, compared to only 87K bytes on the 5-1/4 inch drives on the Model I."* This "new and powerful" machine came with either 32K or 64K of RAM. The price of the 64K model was $3899 and it came with a 12 inch monochrome monitor built in. A 3 disk drive expansion each holding another 8 inch floppy disk was another $2350 and a heavy duty line printer was $1999. The special table to hold this combination of equipment was $350. The modern generation of computer users would be shocked at the primitive specifications of those early machines. There is no way you could even install a modern operating system on those machines. We gradually upgraded as technology improved and we actually became fairly advanced with networking and dumb terminals using a UNIX operating system. Brad McKinley was just out of high school and he was very talented with computer programming. He worked with us for quite awhile trying to develop medical office software that we thought might have commercial possibilities. We never achieved commercial status but I was keeping patient records in a computer database long before it became common to do so. In fact, when some of the faculty members from Oregon Health Sciences University came by on an inspection tour of their preceptorship programs they thought I was way ahead of them at the time concerning computerization of records. When I first switched to the IBM Compatible machines I bought a Compaq brand machine (one of the first "IBM Compatibles") and with it I bought one of the fancy, newly-available hard drives. That hard drive was considered to be really high capacity and held 5 megabytes and cost almost $5000. It was also large and heavy. I was assured at the time that I would never need any more storage capacity. Nowadays you can carry more than a hundred times that capacity in your pocket in a thumb drive for less than $20.

As my kids were growing up I was not home a lot but we managed to get away for camping trips almost every summer. The old school bus we had modified served us well and we found some beautiful camping spots. We preferred to camp in isolated areas and away from designated campgrounds, and this was quite possible in eastern Oregon. One summer we had Toddy's nephew visiting while we were camping in the Wallowa Mountains. Harvey was just a year or two older than our oldest and the kids were having a great time. Kids seem to be programmed to cut things down, chop thing up, throw rocks and dig holes. On this trip they could do it all. We were camped near a fairly small but rapidly moving stream and the kids were chopping down a small dead tree near the stream. I think they were planning to chop it up for campfire wood but it somehow got into the stream and rapidly got away. You can imagine the surprise of some people camped a few hundred yards downstream when our bunch of kids went charging through their camp and on the way through were yelling, "Have you seen a tree go by recently?"

Our boys got started skiing as young teenagers, at first going to Brundage Mountain near McCall, Idaho on a weekend activity bus. They talked the rest of us into trying a weekend of skiing and we were hooked. We tried to get skiing as many weekends as we could manage to get away. We took our old converted school bus up to Goose Creek Store near New Meadows, Idaho and parked it in their RV area.

Several of our friends had RVs up there also so we had good times in the evenings as well as great skiing in the daytime. The school bus had essentially no insulation, and the beds we had made were getting to be too small for the growing kids so we knew we would have to get something else before long. One morning my wife woke up to find that her nightgown had frozen to the wall of the bus with ice from condensation. She decided then and there that there would have to be some changes before the next ski season. The next year we did get a small, but comfortable (and insulated) camping trailer that we used for camping and for a ski house for several more years.

One evening in our "ski house" I was asked to see one of the kids in our RV campground. This child belonged to one of our friends and had a nasty cough. I really didn't have anything to treat this child with but wanted to at least get some relief from coughing so others in his RV could get some sleep. No one in camp seemed to have any cough medicine so I concocted a whisky, lemon juice, and sugar cough syrup that actually tasted pretty good. It would have been fun to have done a "scientific" study on that illness. The contagion period from exposure to symptoms was incredibly short because within minutes all of the kids in camp were showing up at our trailer with coughs. Also a study would have shown that my remedy had been curative within 12 hours because 87.5 percent of the patients, all but the original case, hit the ski slopes in the morning with full vigor. The parents, who were all having a good time, thought the

Family Skiing 1967 - Kathy, Dorin, Don, Alan, Toddy, De Wilda

"epidemic" and the kid's reactions were hilarious. Today I would probably be sued or jailed for child endangerment or abuse.

Every now and then something happens that illustrates a point and becomes a great teaching case. One such incident occurred early in my practice. A wonderful old gentleman came to me with severe abdominal pain. I was able to determine that he had a bowel obstruction and Dr. Tanaka and I operated. At surgery we found that the obstruction was due to cancer of the colon. We were able to relieve the obstruction but we also found that the cancer had spread quite widely and involved the liver. After surgery we confronted the family with the bad news, and as we usually did in this of type situation we advised the family that this man did not have long to live, and that as soon as he was over the immediate effects of the surgery we should tell him what we found so that he could get his affairs in order. The man's wife, one daughter, and both son-in-laws agreed with our recommendations but much to our consternation the other daughter, a teacher, was strongly opposed. Eventually the others succumbed to her wishes in spite of our recommendations. We finally agreed with the family that we would not tell him of his condition even though we disagreed with the decision. We also told the family that we would not actually lie to him and that if he asked specific questions we felt compelled to answer him truthfully. It was one of the hardest several weeks that I have ever experienced because as I made visits to this man I sensed that his total trust in me was rapidly fading. I sensed that he knew his situation and was hurt that we were not open with him. After he died I continued to take care of his family. Jump forward fifteen or so years. The school teacher came to my office and she appeared very apprehensive. She was complaining of a racing and pounding heart, nervousness, trouble sleeping and generally feeling lousy. Patients will tell you a lot about their problems if you take the time and can gently steer the conversation. I was able to learn that she had several cups of coffee at breakfast and some more between classes and at every break plus some more at meals. I was able to get a history of more than twenty cups of coffee per day and was pretty sure that I had identified the problem. I told her that I thought the problem was just too much coffee and told her to cut way down on her coffee intake and come back in a few days after she had obtained an EKG to check for heart disease and some blood tests to rule out anemia and thyroid disease. When she returned she admitted that she felt slightly better but when I told her the lab tests and EKG were normal she acted like she didn't believe it. Again I told her that she had overdosed on caffeine which had caused her symptoms. No matter what I said it didn't seem to soak in. Instead of being relieved she appeared to be getting more apprehensive. Everything I said seemed to pass right by without registering. Finally, in desperation, I blurted out – "Susan (name changed) do you really want to know what is wrong with you?" This time I got her attention and she was now focused. She answered in a hesitating voice "Yes." I said "The problem is that you don't trust me!" She immediately denied my claim stating that she had brought her family to me for years etc. Usually I was quite gentle in my discussions with patients but this time I was firm and said, "Do you remember when we told you that your father was dying and you told us not to tell him because 'if I ever have something bad I don't want to know about it'?" I told her that I remembered almost every word of the conversation of many years ago because it was so difficult for me. I told her that I thought that she thought she had some terrible heart disease and that I was keeping it from her – just like she had instructed me to do with her father. There was a long silence. She finally relaxed and slumped into the chair and meekly said "So that is the problem." She had the intelligence to realize that my argument made sense and immediately accepted my advice. She was a very grateful patient and stayed with me for many more years, even wishing many years after my retirement that I was still available to be her doctor. This story points out several issues: One is that what people say under stressful circumstances can have long term unintended consequences that they may not realize at the conscious level, and Two, there is almost no chance that anyone other than a family doctor who had cared for the family for many years could possibly have recognized the basic problem. In this case there was no need for multiple specialty consultations. *The patient got prompt and lasting relief with the simple reduction of her coffee intake PLUS the realization that you yourself will not trust doctors if you have told the doctor to be dishonest with someone else.* I can imagine how her treatment would have gone had I not pointed out the underlying cause for her distress. She probably would have been seen by cardiologists who would have done expensive tests and who would have had trouble convincing her that her heart was normal. She would probably have been given tranquilizers for her anxiety, and eventually placed on antidepressants. Her distress might not have been resolved even with psychiatric care. I thought that this case was such a good teaching/learning situation that I wrote it up for a contest in the magazine *Medical Economics*. The editors liked the article and printed it after several re-writes by their editorial staff. What came out was so different from what I had submitted that I hardly recognized it as mine. I was so discouraged by having the article so radically changed that I never tried to submit anything else.

In other chapters I have discussed my role in health planning, education, and the evolution of the family medicine specialty. I was also involved some with organized medicine. I served on the Board of Directors of the Oregon Academy of Family Physicians and held an officer position. I served on some busy committees of the OMA (Oregon Medical Association) and spent several years as an Alternate Trustee. I was taking too many trips to Portland and losing too much time out of the office so I had to give up some of my activities. My wife also started insisting that I cut down as my lengthy times away from the office were hurting us financially. I announced that I would no longer be available for officer positions. Some people like to work for years in order to advance in the hierarchy. That seems particularly true in the population centers but I had no interest in titles, I was just interested in serving in order to help medicine keep high standards. In our community most of the doctors were so busy that they didn't want to be on committees or hold offices. In fact if they missed a meeting they were likely to be appointed to positions that they hadn't asked for.

Hospital committee work became progressively more time consuming as outside influences (insurance companies, peer review organizations, welfare, Medicare, Medicaid, etc) all demanded more and more documentation. It seemed that it didn't matter what you did or how you did it as long as the proper buzz words were in the documentation. We spent countless hours challenging adverse rulings because someone hadn't conformed to some new and unannounced requirement. I think it took months of correspondence and phone calls to get approval, after the fact, for a surgeon and the hospital to get paid for a surgery where a lady underwent a previously approved gall bladder surgery, because while looking around the belly after they had removed the gall bladder the doctors found an early ovarian cancer. I believe the patient had already told the doctor to fix anything that needed it. At any rate the doctors removed the ovary and were lucky to have found, and cured, the malignancy at a very early and asymptomatic stage. Payment was denied because the doctors had not conformed to the mandatory waiting period for a procedure that might render a person sterile. I guess the doctors were supposed to wake the patient up, tell her that she had an early cancer and then let her stew for a month or so while the tumor grew before they could do anything about it. Another stupid denial of payment occurred in a previously approved case where as the patient was about to go to sleep he asked the surgeon to fix a small umbilical hernia while he already had the

122

belly open. With the belly already open it only took a couple of minutes to fix the hernia, and the surgeon didn't charge for the extra "bonus" surgery, but the governmental agency involved with payments decreased the amount paid to the hospital because an extra suture was used for an unauthorized operation. Go figure. The cost of getting another operation approved and completed would have been magnitudes more, plus the risk of a second operation. I have heard that the government actually hires independent contractors to search medical records looking for so-called fraud, and do you think that their contracts which give them a percentage cut of any "fraud" penalties awarded might introduce some bias in their investigations? No conflict of interest there – huh!

Hospital administrators come in many flavors. Some are very supportive of their physicians and encourage partnership relationships with hospital personnel. Others consider the doctors to be the enemy. During my many years in Ontario we ran the gamut. Early in my practice a Sister Superior administrator came to Holy Rosary Hospital. The sister was a great PR person who managed to talk a lot of the local businessmen into giving large donations to the hospital. Some of us who had been recently trained and had used some newer technologies were able to convince this Sister Superior to start some modernization. When that sister was rotated out to another job elsewhere in the Order we got another nun as administrator. I don't remember the time line but the first sister mentioned later returned as an administrator. We don't know what happened but she was a changed person. She was no longer the cheerful upbeat person we had known. Modernization slowed down. She was suspicious and secretive. She did all of the hiring herself and when she discussed salary levels with new nurses it was a one on one discussion. The nurse was then advised to not discuss her salary with anyone else. This nun bugged the nurses' station on the Medical Floor (this was before transistors - such devices were made with vacuum tubes) and probably also the doctor's dressing room in surgery. She would secretly monitor the entrance to the hospital at shift change time to see if any employee was a few minutes late coming to work. Morale dropped to new low levels throughout the hospital and it was beginning to adversely affect patient care. Doctors and nurses felt that the situation was becoming intolerable and formed a Physician/Nurse Liaison Committee which met outside the hospital because we didn't know where we could safely meet inside the hospital – none of us knew where there might be electronic bugs. We corresponded with the Sister House in Kenosha, Wisconsin and told them what was happening and requested their help. There were many letters and many phone calls, and unbeknownst to us some of the information we provided was gathered and used to provide ammunition for some of their own internal squabbles. We were finally able to get some changes made and the clearly sick Nun was finally removed. It really isn't easy for doctors and nurses to get a nun fired who is the administrator of a Catholic Hospital.

After the above problem was resolved we got our first non-nun administrator. Chuck Smith, the administrator at the Nyssa hospital moved over to Ontario and assumed the administration role. Chuck was well known to us as many of us had hospital privileges in Nyssa as well as Ontario and we also knew him as an excellent nurse anesthetist. Chuck was just what we needed to get things moving in the right direction. He was well informed on new advances in medical technology and helped us modernize as fast as budgets would allow. As best as I can determine the only real fault Chuck had as an administrator was that he overreacted to the previous autocracy and became too democratic. He involved the head nurses in too many accounting and administrative duties in an attempt to get them to help with management decisions. This frequently made the nurses feel uncomfortable as that was not what they had been trained for and many wanted to have more time for patient care. When Chuck developed serious health problems and had to step down after about seven years we had another administrative nightmare to deal with. The hospital hired an administrator from Eastern Idaho who seemed OK at first but it soon became apparent that his management style was foreign to our way of thinking. He tended to store every bit of information he was able to glean about the various doctors apparently so he could "have something on them." He made his top aides insulate him from contact with almost everyone. He started to design medical clinics within the hospital to be used by hospital-hired physicians and had plans to start excluding the private physicians who had served the hospital well for years. This and other information that came out much later seemed to indicate that he had plans to get the hospital away from the Catholic order and convert it to a private, for profit hospital. He wouldn't let employees from different departments eat with each other – apparently fearing some sort of conspiracy. He treated the nurses badly and they reached a point that they unionized and actually went on strike. During the strike the patients were cared for by supervisory level nurses and one day I met the head nurse supervisor in the hallway and she expressed concern for the head nurse from the Critical Care Unit. I had been caring for that nurse and I was concerned that she was overly fatigued from long work hours and this was not good for her chronic heart condition. During the hallway conversation the nurse supervisor became more and more fidgety and when I asked her what was wrong she blurted out that if she was seen talking to a doctor she would lose her job. Well, when a doctor and a nurse can't talk to each other in the hospital, and aren't allowed to discuss care of patients you know things have gotten out of hand. The Nurse/Physician Liaison Committee had already been re-formed. All of the head nurses put their jobs on the line and signed grievance statements knowing that if they did not get administrative changes they would be fired. Many of the doctors documented their concerns and all this time communications were underway with the Sister House in Kenosha, Wisconsin. The hospital board of directors, which had been reduced pretty much to a name only status, became active again and they joined the battle. It was a very tense time and there was great relief when that administrator was let go. I don't know the figures but I suspect that the hospital lost a bunch of money in that fiasco. The board was much more careful in picking the next administrator and hired Dave Goode who was a solid and stable administrator for about ten years before leaving Ontario to assume a higher role in the Catholic Health Care system. Dave left not long before I retired so I really didn't have much time with the administrators that followed. Over the years Holy Rosary Hospital was an excellent place to work and the patients were well treated.

During my first several years of practice, head injuries were real anxiety provoking situations. In those days it was fairly common to have concussions and more serious head injuries from car accidents, horse accidents, athletic injuries, and industrial accidents. We only had skull x-rays and spinal taps (looking for blood in the spinal fluid) as relatively benign diagnostic tools. MRIs and CAT scans to help us evaluate the severity of the problem had not been invented yet and we had to rely heavily on clinical findings. To make things worse the only neurosurgeon in the whole Boise-Treasure Valley area was overworked and was often trying to get stress relief at the Elks club in Boise. This made it difficult to get consultations and also made the quality of his advice somewhat problematic. I remember quite vividly one time I had him on the phone to discuss what I thought to be a severe concussion case but I was concerned that it might be something worse. After discussing the problem for a short time his advice to me was, "It sounds like you are doing all you can do. If the patient is still alive in three days send him over!" That wasn't exactly the type of help I was looking for. Nowadays an injury like that would have an immediate helicopter ride to Boise where there are many neurosurgeons (and they are all busy). One particularly bad head injury occurred on a patient of mine. She was a dynamic go-getter who held many jobs and on this occasion she was driving a school bus to some evening school event. She stepped out of the bus to check a tire that she thought might be getting low and was hit by a passing motorist. When she got into the hospital it was apparent that she had a severe head injury and was in critical condition. Again the only neurosurgeon in the valley was unavailable and I immediately got Dr. Tanaka to help me. He had spent some time in his surgical residency on the neurosurgical wards so at least he had been exposed to this type of injury. It was apparent that the patient was losing ground steadily and Dr. Tanaka and I both knew that the patient would be dead within a few hours if we didn't relieve the pressure on her brain. Dr. Tanaka was finally able to contact Dr. Hal Brown in Nampa, who was a neurologist, and he concurred with Gus that we had to put burr holes into her skull immediately. We had the maintenance shop in the hospital bring up some drills and bits that we could sterilize and took the patient into surgery. Dr. Brown arrived at the hospital just as we were starting the surgery to provide us with moral support. The patient was deeply comatose so no anesthesia was needed. We made a scalp incision and drilled holes where we had been instructed to place them. As we penetrated the inner plate of the skull there was a great spurt of blood, obviously under considerable pressure, and the patient started to wake up. She had a stormy post operative course but she lived. It took a long period of rehab before she could function adequately enough to care for herself, but at least she was alive. We both felt sort of smug about our crude neurosurgery until I read about a head injury in a cowboy near the Alvord Ranch east of Steens Mountain in southeast Oregon. The book "In the Shadow of the Steens" had been written by Leilani Davis (I had taken care of her husband when he was in high school) and in the book was a reference to a letter from the late 1800s describing a cowboy's severe head injury. Somewhere near the Alvord Ranch the cowboy had fallen or been kicked by a horse and was unconscious. He had been taken by a horse drawn farm wagon to the nearest doctor – a two day trip to Burns, Oregon. The letter mentioned that it was probably a good thing that the patient was unconscious the whole time as a two day trip in a wagon wouldn't have been any fun while awake. The doctor in Burns put in burr holes and the patient was back at work in fairly short time. It wasn't stated but I would guess that the doctor had served in the Civil War and had dealt with severe head injuries before and probably had a trephine made for the job in his kit. Anyhow we saved a life but the doctor in Burns had done the same surgery almost one hundred years before we did and under rougher conditions so we weren't as pioneering as we had thought. As we got new technologies (MRI, CAT, and Nuclear Scans) our diagnostic capabilities improved dramatically. New neurosurgeons moved into the valley and I finally felt greatly relieved to be able to quickly refer these difficult problems.

Another case that made me a bit uncomfortable was a high school student who rolled his car on a steep hillside and wound up in the hospital with a nasty compound fracture dislocation of his ankle. We had no orthopedic surgeon at the time and all of the general surgeons were out of town. One look showed a very cyanotic blue foot so it was imperative to get the dislocation reduced quickly in order to save the foot. I got the patient into surgery and under anesthesia was able to get the dislocation reduced and fortunately the foot started to pink up. I then got busy scrubbing and picking lava rock debris out of his ankle joint where the articulating surface of the tibia had dirt ground in to it. Before I was done the nurses who had been trying to locate an orthopedic surgeon for me finally located Dr. Baranco in Caldwell. I broke scrub, talked to him on the phone and was expecting him to offer to take over but he assured me that I was doing everything that should be done and if the patient was not doing well in six weeks he would see him. As I was hanging up he gave me one more bit of advice. He said, "Oh, by the way, be sure to tell the patient that he is going to have a bad ankle for the rest of his life!" I guess I should have felt comforted but I really wasn't. I closed the wound and put on a cast and the patient did OK.

In an earlier chapter I mentioned the doctors that I recalled being in practice when I moved to the Vale/Ontario area. For a long time we had great difficulty attracting new doctors to the area and many of those who practiced here were seriously overworked. The arrival of Emergency Physicians was a big help. Our emergency physicians evolved from contracting groups that rotated in from elsewhere to a local autonomous group. A federal program was set up to serve the migrant population. This program has gone through several iterations and is still operating. Doctors in that program rotated through – some putting in time to qualify for citizenship or to qualify for relief of student loans for practicing in an underserved area. We gradually got some new physicians in various specialties and gradually had the specialties of OB/GYN, ENT, Urology, Pediatrics, Orthopedics and General Surgery fairly well covered. While we got some new primary care physicians in Family Practice and Internal Medicine we continued to be short handed in those fields. One physician who was in the early batches of Emergency Physicians from the San Francisco area became enamored with a local nurse and eventually married her. Dr. Fred Stark had been an Army physician who was high enough in rank that he was assigned to increasing amounts of desk assignments. He did not want to be removed from front line crisis medicine so he moonlighted on weekends with the Mangold emergency medicine group and rotated several times to Ontario. He is a brilliant physician who has achieved Board status in Internal Medicine, Infectious Disease, and Allergy and Immunology. When he left the Army he set up a high tech research company in California and then spent some time doing research in England. He eventually returned to Ontario to practice medicine and to raise his children in a community he felt was a good place to live. He thrives on difficult challenges and is a real asset to the community. The younger surgeons that moved in after Drs. Gus Tanaka and Lester Scott retired formed a great team. They – Drs. Babij, Spokas, and Tesnohlidek, - have covered the community well and are serving as off-campus preceptors for a surgical rotation for the OHSU Family Medicine Residents. For a long time we were very short on pediatricians. We were fortunate to get Dr. Robert Thornfeldt to come out of retirement and serve many more years in our community. He had been an outstanding pioneer neonatologist/pediatrician in Portland for twenty four years and had moved to our area for a change of climate because of his chronic respiratory disease. He served us well for another eighteen years before retiring again. Doctors have come and some have gone but generally we have had high quality physicians in our community.

My brother, Farrington Daniels Jr., graduated from Harvard Medical School in WWII and had served in the army at the end of the war. After he was discharged from the service he took an Internal Medicine residency at Cornell and later a Dermatology residency at the University of Oregon Medical School in Portland. He wound up at Cornell University Medical School on the faculty of the Dermatology Division and eventually became chairman of the department. When he found out that in my "General Practice" I was treating lots of warts and other benign skin lesions he gave some instruction in the new and evolving treatment of Cryosurgery. His associate and good friend at Cornell, Doug Torre, was a pioneer in cryotherapy (freezing treatments) for skin lesions and he had developed a device that simplified the treatment of skin lesions. The device made the treatment much more controllable than just dipping a cotton swab into liquid nitrogen in a foam plastic cup and applying it to the lesion. My brother convinced me to buy this new equipment, which I did, and I soon became very busy using the device. I had the newest and best equipment in the whole valley for some time. After several years of using liquid nitrogen for skin lesions I developed a fairly wide ranging reputation. One day I had a new patient who was literally covered with keratotic skin lesions that she wanted treated. I noted that she was from California and asked her how she happened to come to me. She didn't say much other than that she was visiting a long time friend and had been recommended to me. I kept treating her on that visit until she had had enough for the day and I forgot about the episode until a couple of years later when she showed up again and wanted more treatments. As I was treating multiple lesions we were just visiting and I mentioned that even though I had better equipment than most doctors I thought that she should be able to find a dermatologist in her area of California that could take care of her. With a sly grin she responded, "Yes, there are dermatologists near me that could do the job BUT I can buy a round trip plane ticket to Boise, visit my friend here for a week, get treated by you and still spend less money than it would cost me to have the lesions treated at home." I knew that many doctors charged a lot more than I did but I began to think that maybe I wasn't charging enough.

My contact with lawyers and the legal system over the years was both interesting and stressful. The first time I recall being asked to testify in court concerned a child who had been severely abused by her parents. I had delivered the child and on follow-up newborn examinations I had been concerned that the child had not been gaining weight. On one exam I had observed some bruises and what appeared to be burns on her skin. I fortunately was able to convince the mother to admit the

129

child to the hospital for evaluation and we found that the child had cigarette burns on her body and multiple fractures in different stages of healing. In the hospital the child quickly became less irritable and started gaining weight. We found no evidence of metabolic disease to account for the broken bones so we felt that we had a case of what was being newly described in the medical and legal literature as "Battered Child Syndrome." The Oregon Statutes at that time had not addressed the problem as such and there was no precedent to bring charges under the title of "Battered Child Syndrome" so the District Attorney, Cliff Looney, had to be innovative in attempting to prosecute the parents. Of course I was the primary witness in the case describing the history and findings of the horrific injuries that the child had sustained. We had photographs and x-rays which were pretty self explanatory. I was not used to testifying and was definitely stressed and nervous. During my testimony I was trying to introduce information from the literature indicating that this condition was starting to be recognized as a specific syndrome. I made the mistake of mentioning that in some states this syndrome was being legally recognized. WOW- the judge, Jeff Dorrah, just about came unglued. The judge had been a military man and had a reputation of being hard on witnesses – a trait I was not aware of at the time. He yelled at me and asked what law school I had gone to and let me know in no uncertain terms that I was not qualified to say anything about legal cases etc., etc., etc. Of course I was rattled but the case had been adequately made and both parents spent jail time. I followed the child for many years through foster homes and adoption. She had some lifelong problems related to her childhood injuries and when she was an adult and finally learned of her childhood abuse she exhibited considerable denial.

Another time I had contact with attorneys was related to a delivery that I had done. My patient came to me after the delivery and showed me a letter she had received from her insurance company. Her well-known insurance company had sent her a letter indicating that I had charged too much for her prenatal care and delivery. It also stated that if she incurred any legal expense trying to recover some of my fee, they would help with her legal expenses. My patient's husband was working for a government agency and they had moved fairly frequently so she knew what charges were elsewhere. She thought my charges were very reasonable and instead of being upset with me she thought I should know what the insurance company was doing. I had been crusading throughout my career to improve the quality of medical care in small towns and trying to attract family physicians to small communities. I contacted the OMA (Oregon Medical Association) and the OAFP (Oregon Academy of Family Physicians) and both were outraged and we all agreed that we should challenge the insurance company's conduct. In those days doctors were not supposed to know what other doctors were charging. If we discussed fees with other doctors it was called collusion and that was a no-no. With the help of my friend Cliff Looney, now in private legal practice instead of the DA's office, and with the blessings of the medical societies we filed a suit against the insurance company. Having filed the suit we were able to enter a discovery process and I was able to get enough information to determine that the insurance company was happy to pay specialists in my area more than I had charged, and they were also willing to pay family physicians more than I had charged if they lived in larger communities. This was clearly a slap in the face of the small town doctors, with the big and powerful insurance company telegraphing the message that small town family doctors were not as good as big city doctors or specialists and should not be paid as much. I was highly incensed by that behavior which could make it even harder for us to attract doctors to practice in small towns than it already was. I never liked the argument that doctors in big cities should be paid more than small town doctors because their cost of living was higher. I had to pay as much for my supplies and equipment as the city doctors did. Maybe our houses cost less but most of us lived in modest houses. I also didn't think that the cost of country club dues and high priced cars characteristic of many city doctors should be considered in the cost of living formula. A lot of people thought I was totally off my rocker for taking on a big insurance company because the insurance company had a lot of money and high powered lawyers and could literally chew me up and spit me out, but I had a strong sense of righteous indignation. Behind the scenes the medical societies were cheering me on and helping me to obtain data and statistics for my battle. My biggest cost was time out of the office preparing for court. My attorney and I went to Portland to consult with another attorney and as the court date was approaching, the insurance company publicly made a change in their national policy of discriminating against small town doctors. The case became moot and of course I got nothing because we didn't actually go to court. After the suit was dropped my attorney told me that he thought that "insurance company X" at least now knew where Ontario, Oregon was located and that they knew the name of Dorin

Daniels. I know there were other howls of anguish all around the country but I think my suit was a significant part of the reason they changed their policy.

I was only sued once in my forty plus years in medicine. This suit had absolutely no merit but it caused me a lot of grief and stress. One morning I was called in to help one of the surgeons with an emergency operation. (I had been scheduled to help this surgeon on an elective case that was being preempted by this emergency.) The patient had come in to the hospital during the night with gastro-intestinal bleeding and had been watched closely with the thought that she might need surgical intervention, but seemed to be stabilizing so was being treated conservatively. I think it was around 6:30 a.m. when she suddenly had another massive bleeding episode and went in to shock. Help from the emergency room, anesthesiologist, and nurses coming on shift and those still working all pitched in and provided superb care and rapidly got her ready for surgery. She was rushed into the operating room where the surgeon rapidly got the bleeding stopped just as I got to the hospital to assist him. I helped close the incision but my total involvement was only a short time. This woman had a stormy course and her shock episode was severe enough to have left her with some brain damage. It was a sad case of a bad outcome but the care she got was superb. In fact it was a tribute to the doctors and nurses that she survived at all. I thought nothing more of the case until several months later I was served papers indicating that I was being sued for $200,000,000.00. That's right – 200 million dollars. Of course I was shocked and immediately called the OMA for advice and they were shocked at the amount of the suit. I soon found out that six doctors and the hospital were all being sued each for 200 million dollars making it I believe the highest claim for malpractice in the State of Oregon to that point in time. To make things worse the suit for each of us was for 100 million dollars general damages and 100 million dollars punitive damages. For those who don't know it, the punitive damages are not covered by insurance. I knew that there should be no reason for me to lose this suit as I didn't think I could have been found to have done anything wrong, but the thought of being successfully sued has a very negative effect on one's disposition. As I read the charges I vacillated from incredulous to angry to shocked to almost laughing because the charges were so ridiculous. The papers served were signed by a local attorney. The wording and grammar seemed to be of a grade school level. The charge that I had deliberately wanted to see the patient suffer, as justification for the punitive portion of the claim, was so outlandish as to be laughable if it weren't so frightening. It soon became apparent that the attorney calling the shots was a high powered attorney from southern California who had been involved with several high profile cases. When my turn came to be deposed I was understandably nervous. The attorney from California looked the part of a sleazy, obese, crook from a gangster movie. He asked me several questions and it was quickly apparent to him that I was not guilty of any wrongdoing so he changed tactics. He tried to twist me upside down and backwards verbally and I could see that he was trying to get me to incriminate someone else. He buttered me up saying that I appeared to be a good doctor but he kept trying to get me to tell him who else had really done something wrong. I felt strongly that everyone involved had acted promptly and properly to every phase of the patient's care and he finally dismissed me. A month or so later I got a letter stating that they would dismiss Dr. Daniels from the case if he would pay them something like $10,000. That sure sounded better than 200 million dollars but I was incensed – to me that was out and out blackmail and I refused the offer. My attorneys (local and insurance company) agreed that I shouldn't sign that document and they were also upset by that tactic. A month or two later I got another letter offering to release me from the suit if I would sign the enclosed statement, which in essence stated that I agreed that there was reason to have brought suit against each and every party named. Again I was furious – I wasn't going to sign something like that which would essentially incriminate everyone involved with the patient's care – including myself. My attorneys agreed that I should not sign that document either. As the trial date got closer I got another letter – this time offering to let me off of the case if I would sign a document agreeing not to counter sue. I was furious at their tactics again but on advice of my attorneys I signed the papers. The attorneys told me that I didn't have a ghost of a chance of successfully countersuing so "sign and be done with it!" That episode was very stressful because you can never be quite sure how juries will react in sympathy cases and any award could have been devastating to me. I was not a wealthy man and could have been totally wiped out with even a small judgment. I did not have a good taste in my mouth concerning the legal system for a long time. The hospital made some sort of a settlement, not because there was any merit to the case but because in the interest of accuracy a few notes were made on the chart later that were actual corrections to the sequence of events during the emergency but it was feared that they could be interpreted in court as changes to the record. The other doctors were gradually dropped from the suit except Dr. Phillips, the internist who was most involved with her care, and he finally won after a lengthy trial. Everyone was sorry for the woman but we were all upset at the viciousness with which we were attacked without justification.

Because both my wife and I were having health problems we started thinking about retirement. I had had a scare early in my practice with a polio-like illness that left one leg weak for several years. I had had several acute ruptured disc episodes in my low back and neck with excruciating pain or other neurological problems. I got excellent surgical relief in most cases. I had had a viral pneumonia that had been given a presumptive diagnosis of carcinoma which fortunately was not correct. I developed diabetes which gradually went through the usual course of diet controlled, to pills, and then to the point that I needed to be on insulin. When I started on pills for diabetes I had to stop flying. A few years later they changed the regulations to allow flying if the diabetes was adequately controlled on pills and I flew again for awhile. When I started insulin I was again out of flying. Eventually the FAA allowed flight status on insulin if certain criteria were met and I flew again for a short time. The requirements for special tests were expensive and the medical certification was of such a short duration that I finally stopped flying entirely.

My wife had been having heart trouble for many years before we considered retirement. She had developed a floppy mitral valve which bothered her and she had associated irregular heart rhythms. Usually this condition was not considered really serious and she was diagnosed with early experimental ultrasound equipment at the medical school. That early ultrasound equipment took up a whole wall in a research lab at the school and the results were hard to interpret. Her sister had the same problem and her valve actually ruptured requiring emergency heart surgery with valve replacement, so we knew that not all cases were minor. As the years went on my wife developed frequent episodes of chest pain and required multiple heart surgeries. I had been hoping to practice another five or more years and actually thought I could not afford to retire. We had not done well with investments but we did own the farm property and my wife convinced me that

134

retirement was doable (even though we would have to be very frugal) and that she wanted to have some play time while she was still able. Our group had already sold our clinic building to the hospital and Dr Tanaka had already retired so I arranged to sell my office equipment and supplies to the hospital with hopes that they could attract and set up another doctor in my place. I had already arranged to work for a *locum tenens* group so that I could work on occasion filling in for doctors needing relief and I also arranged to do some part time work for a local acute care clinic. In both those settings I incurred no costs for overhead or insurance so I was pretty much able to pick my times to work after I closed the office in May of 1994.

Sliver Time - House Call On Niece Sarah - Nephew David Observing

Dorin in 6th Grade - Nakoma School Orchestra

Dad At Cave Point - About Five Miles From The D6 Cabin - Surprised By Wave

Watermelon Seed Spitting Contest - D6 Cabin Beach 1965 - I'm The Fat One At My Heaviest

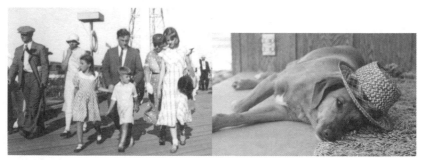

Daniels Family At The Chicago World's Fair - 1934   Our Dog "Pat" In Her Retirement Years

Miscellaneous Family Pictures

Pregnant Ladies and Newborns

I always enjoyed working with young families, so dealing with mothers and babies was an important part of my practice. My University of Chicago Medical School exposure to obstetrics was somewhat limited. As a third year medical student in 1955 I had the usual exposure to obstetrics and gynecology, consisting of lectures, hospital rounds with the professors, and observation of deliveries, and the unpleasant task of removing stitches from private and tender places about five days after deliveries. Chicago Lying-In Hospital, which was part of the University of Chicago complex, had been way ahead of its time 50 or so years before my medical school class arrived. The famous old doctors who still ruled the department had sort of rested on their laurels, and were many years behind the rest of the nation in several aspects of their specialty. They had been slow to adopt shorter hospital stays following deliveries, and they had not adopted dissolving sutures in some delivery procedures (hence the role of the medical student in removing sutures.) The medical student's role in deliveries was limited pretty much to following the patient in labor, and then observing the delivery. In the delivery room, the Chief Resident would observe the Assistant Resident who was actually doing the delivery, and the Intern, followed by the nursing student, the midwife trainee, and the medical student – in that order – all observing. It was, for the medical student, sort of like being at a basketball game, high in the bleachers, in a seat behind a support pillar. I felt that we might have learned more if we had been issued periscopes.

As noted in the Alaska chapter, I spent the last six months of medical school at a TB hospital in Seward, Alaska. I was more than a bit surprised, and challenged, when I was informed by Dr Phillips, the thoracic surgeon who ran the hospital, that I was expected to do all of the deliveries! This announcement occurred on my first day in Alaska, and it did not instill in me a high degree of confidence, as I did not feel adequately qualified for the assignment. Fortunately, we had some very experienced nurses on staff who skillfully talked me through my first few deliveries in Alaska.

I arrived in Portland in the summer of 1956 after my Alaska experience to start my internship at St. Vincent's Hospital where I received excellent training in Obstetrics. Dr. J. Oppie McCall was the obstetrical specialist we chose to deliver our third child. He was highly respected and was well known for his extreme skill with forceps. We frequently referred to him as "the wizard of the forceps." During my two years in Portland I spent many sessions with him using the baby manikin and model pelvis to practice a wide variety of normal and abnormal deliveries. Not many years after this excellent training the use of forceps was discouraged, as the medical/legal atmosphere became so oppressive. Later, even the residents in training for the specialty of obstetrics were not given the forceps training that I had benefited from, because it was legal suicide if a baby had any problem at all and forceps had been used. Many specialists were trained to go to an immediate c-section for problems that might easily have been resolved with the skillful use of forceps. In fact I delivered many breech presentations because I had been well trained in the technique, and in the proper use of forceps. Later it became standard practice to do c-sections on most breech deliveries. In my estimation far too many c-sections were performed because the newer obstetricians were not trained in forceps, and were afraid to use them. In Portland I got as much OB exposure as I could. In fact it was one of the best rotations because we worked 24 hours on and had 24 hours off. This was an improvement on hours as we usually worked 16 to 18 hours a day with no time off on the other services. In my second year of training in Portland, a General Practice Residency, I spent several months in the unwed mother facility. At that time many high school girls from around the state who got pregnant (not common in those days) were sent to the Catholic Charities Home for continued education, prenatal care and delivery. After delivery they adopted their children out and went back to their homes, supposedly to an unknowing community. In this setting I learned how attached and dependent young pregnant women became toward their doctors. In fact it made me aware of the awesome responsibility a physician has with his patient.

When I went to Vale, Oregon in the summer of 1958 to start my medical practice, most of the deliveries for the whole area had been done by Dr Belnap who had been there for many years and had delivered thousands of babies through the war years. He was cutting down on his practice, and a lot of the deliveries were being switched to a younger associate, Dr. Burdic, who got very busy delivering babies. Dr. Sanders, also in the Ontario Clinic had done quite a few deliveries but was no longer taking obstetrical patients. I was getting an increasing number of pregnant women in my practice and I was using the hospitals in Nyssa and in Ontario. Some patients had a strong preference for one hospital or the other and as I got busier I ran into some problems with logistics: Ontario, Nyssa, and Vale formed a triangle on the map, each leg being fifteen to twenty miles, and communication in those days was limited. We didn't have cell phones or radios so I was really out of touch until I got to one hospital or another where I could get to a phone. On one occasion I recall having a lady in labor in each hospital at the same time and was trying to decide from the nurse's description which to head for first. I finally decided to go to Ontario first, and when I arrived there I got a frantic call from Nyssa saying that they needed me right now. I headed for Nyssa and got there to find that another doctor had already delivered the baby for me, so I headed back to Ontario where I found that they had called another doctor to deliver that baby.

As I was getting busier I was faced with another factor that increased my obstetrical load tremendously. Dr. Burdic had decided to go back to school for training in psychiatry. I had already been getting Ontario patients by that time, because of the overload that Drs. Burdic and Belnap had experienced. It became apparent that if I was to have a rapidly increasing obstetrical load, it would make sense to be closer to the primary hospital, so those factors weighed heavily on our decision to move from Vale to Ontario. I had been spending far too many hours traveling to and from hospitals, making rounds usually twice a day and being on the road often three or more hours per day.

When I moved to Ontario my obstetrical practice exploded. I soon became the doctor who delivered the most babies and it put me in a rather uncomfortable position. There were many times that I wanted to have consultations but didn't have easy access to specialists. Dr. Belnap would help when he could but his health was failing. I was considerably relieved later when Dr. Sigurdson arrived in town. He was a newly trained OB/GYN specialist and he was a great addition to the community. He took a lot of the obstetrical load and gradually reached a point where he was doing more deliveries than I was. We developed a good working relationship and he was always very helpful when I had a problem. I had him do all of my C-sections, except when he was unavailable at which point I got excellent help from the younger general surgeons, Drs. Tanaka and Scott. The general surgeons would not enter into decisions as to who needed a C-section, but they trusted my judgment and provided superb help.

When Dr. Sigurdson was new in town, and was not yet well known, he was covering my deliveries one day while I was out of town. One of my patients was progressing rapidly in labor and he was called to deliver the baby. As he quickly washed his hands and put on his gown the patient asked him "Who are you?" to which he jokingly replied "I'm the janitor – they call me when they can't find the doctor." She was not comforted by that comment, and the Catholic nun in charge of the floor was left sputtering as she tried very hard to convince the patient that he was really a doctor, and actually a specialist. We laugh when we recall that incident but I don't think the patient really appreciated the humor.

Early in my practice a very pushy, domineering, young preacher brought his wife to me for a pregnancy evaluation. She was several months along at the time. He wanted to participate in ALL aspects of the prenatal examination, which was a bit unusual, but the wife appeared to accept his wishes. Everything appeared normal and he then announced that he was going to deliver the baby himself at home and wondered if I would check the wife and baby after the delivery. This was not a situation that I had anticipated, and I explained to him that I was not comfortable with home deliveries because I had seen too many emergencies arise without warning that I was uncomfortable being so far from the hospital. (I was in Vale at the time and almost twenty miles from the hospital). He was so adamant that he was going to deliver the baby himself, whether I helped or not, that I agreed on the strict condition that if the patient developed problems there was to be no argument with my decisions on care from that point on. He agreed and several months later I started getting phone calls from him about his wife's progress in labor. He was trying to give me all of the details including the status of her dilatation. I didn't feel real comfortable with his descriptions, as he had no training or experience. I recalled that it took me several hundred labor observations before I felt comfortable with judging the degree of cervical dilatation. As many hours went by I sensed that the poor lady was approaching total exhaustion and probably getting a bit dehydrated. Also some of the cockiness of the husband was beginning to mellow a bit. I suggested that he bring her to the office where I could check her and he reluctantly agreed. My exam revealed that she was not likely to deliver normally, that she needed some relief from pain, and needed fluids. I also reminded him that he was no longer in charge, and that he had agreed to abide by my decisions. He agreed to take her to the hospital where we determined that her pelvis was too small for normal delivery. As soon as the decision was made that I would take over her care I could see extreme gratitude in the patient's eyes – she had had enough of the husband and home delivery scenario. We did a C-section and got a good baby, a happy mother, and a rather subdued father. They did not stay in Vale for very long and I wonder to this day what became of that marriage.

Most deliveries go well, and everybody is happy, in contrast to the bad accident or serious illness that presents severe and unhappy challenges for the patient and their families. However, when problems arise in pregnancy or delivery they can turn into serious emergencies quickly. I was very lucky throughout my career that I had been well trained, that I took extra training as the years went by, and that I almost always had good help available. I feel good that in many cases my skill and experience allowed me to intervene successfully and prevent disasters. It has been very rewarding to have patients, years after an emergency situation, thank me for my services. I recently was at a banquet where a lady came up to me and very emotionally thanked me for saving her baby thirty plus years before and said she had been planning to write me all those years. She had developed what we call a mal presentation, where the baby was not able to be delivered normally. The baby was showing some distress and I had arranged for an emergency C-section In addition to the abnormal position, the umbilical cord was wrapped several times around the baby's neck and also had a knot in it, which further compounded the situation. The baby was quite distressed after delivery, but fortunately we had a well trained anesthetist who was able to get the baby's airway open. The baby was transferred to Boise for special neonatal care and was able to come home in a week or two and did well. Thirty plus years after the incident it is very touching to be so profusely and emotionally thanked by both the patient and her husband for my part in getting a good baby who became valedictorian of her high school class.

I think all of us experience situations that we recall for years with flashes of memory that makes us smile and have fuzzy warm feelings, no matter what you are doing at the time. One such situation for me occurred almost thirty years ago when I happened to be on obstetrical call for the hospital. (We had a rotation of all the doctors who delivered babies so that the nurses could find a doctor when an unattended patient needed attention.) A very attractive pregnant lady came to the hospital in advanced labor. She was from out of town and was driving to a new job in another state when she went into labor and stopped at our hospital. She was obviously well educated and self assured. As I was examining her and preparing her for delivery she informed me that she planned to adopt the baby out, and that she intended to leave the hospital within twenty four hours of delivery. At that time the usual hospital stay was three to five days. We were faced with an unusual request and a very short timeline in which to find an adopting family and get legal papers prepared. The hospital administrator, the hospital chaplain, and I went into a huddle to try to meet the challenge. After some discussion we thought of a solution – if our potential parents would be willing. We had all been impressed at how similar in appearance and personality this patient was to a nurse we knew who had not been able to have her own children and who after considerable waiting had finally adopted a child. The administrator or the chaplain called the prospective adoptive mother and said something like – "Mary, (name changed), would you consider adopting another baby?" After a bit of discussion she gave a tentative "yes" and asked when she was to expect the baby. You can imagine her sputtering response when she was told "tomorrow"! We got an attorney to quickly do the legal work. Today it would probably take several months of state supervision and perhaps several foster homes before a child could be finally adopted. I delivered a good baby, the mother left the next day after signing papers, and we kept the baby in the hospital a day or two longer so the new adoptive parents could get prepared. My wife and I took the baby to our home, just outside of the city limits, where the new parents met us so that they could legitimately say that they had to go out of town to get their new baby. Maybe once every year or two I run into the adoptive mother and get a nice hug.

Over the twenty-eight or so years that I did deliveries I estimate the total number at over 3500. In my busiest years I delivered approximately 175 each year. Accurate counts are impossible as sometimes another doctor would deliver one of mine or I would deliver one of his. When Dr. Sigurdson was out of town I would deliver many of his patients. Dr. Mann, an excellent family doctor in our clinic, also did some obstetrics and was of great help covering for me on my many trips out of town while I served on many committees. With that large a volume it is not surprising that I saw a lot of

142

emergencies and abnormalities. Obstetrical problems can go from routine to panic mode in a matter of minutes. Babies can present with unexpected congenital anomalies that can turn a happy event into a tragedy. Fetal infections and premature labor were constant threats to be dealt with. Some of the more bizarre situations are of medical interest but details would best be described in another setting.

There are many large families in the Vale and Ontario areas. This is due in large part to the fact that there are a lot of Catholics and a lot of LDS (Mormon) families. The Mormon ladies were instructed to have large families for religious reasons, and the Catholics were taught that birth control was wrong. The result was essentially the same – BIG families. At one particularly busy delivery period I recall the nun in charge of the OB service running around busily and muttering "I think the Mormons and the Catholics are having a race, and I think the Mormons are winning." It was not unusual for me to deliver four or five babies to a family. It was not unusual to deliver twenty or so grandchildren to a family I had cared for. I even delivered second generations of babies – I had delivered their mothers years previously. I delivered two babies to a couple, both of whom I had delivered. One day I delivered a baby boy and a baby girl at the Ontario hospital. The parents of the babies did not know each other, and the babies didn't know each other until years later when they had a chance meeting at a college event and started dating. The conversation over several dates is reported to be something like "where are you from?" and "what is your birth date?" until they both figured out that they had been born the same day, in the same hospital, and delivered by the same doctor (me). They fell in love, got married, and the situation got Paul Harvey News recognition. I heard the broadcast and thought it was a nice story even if Paul did mispronounce my name. I recently met the couple at his father's memorial services and found them to be an absolutely lovely couple. It is sad that it took his father's death for me to meet them as adults. His father was a blind attorney with his own incredible story of accomplishments in the face of adversity.

As I write these stories at age eighty one I am reminded of how lucky I was to have practiced in a small town and to have been involved with the lives of so many good families. I recently attended an Eagle Scout Award ceremony as a representative of our local historical society. I was asked to attend because the historical society had supported the scout in a project involving pioneer cemeteries for which he received a

143

merit badge. I didn't know much more about the circumstances or about the scout until I got to the ceremony where I found that I had delivered the scout's mother, his father, and many of the relatives who were attending.

Delivering babies for the most part was a fun part of my practice. It was much more fun as a family practitioner than it would have been as an OB specialist as I dealt with the entire family, and watched them grow up. It was a sad day when I was forced to give up the delivery aspect of my practice. On very short notice I was informed that if I continued to deliver babies I would have to pay an extra $40,000 per year in malpractice insurance premiums, and at that time I was down to thirty or so deliveries a year, many of which were welfare or indigent patients, so it was economically impossible for me to continue. As expected, from that point on my practice gradually drifted away from young families and more to the elderly. The good part of the switch was that I didn't have to go out so much at night, and I finally realized how much of the time I had been fatigued.

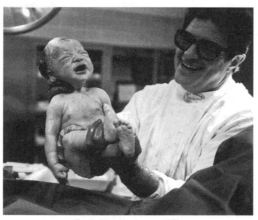

Really New Newborn c. 1979

Health Planning
Goals, Frustrations, and Bureaucratic Interventions.

In the 1970s and 1980s there was a great interest in "Health Planning." There was a race by many individuals and organizations to seek federal grant money for a variety of projects. The federal government was also trying to gain more control over the practice of medicine and the running of hospitals. Somehow I was maneuvered into accepting positions (all volunteer) in a variety of planning committees and seemed to be elevated from one position to another over a several year period. Most of the state committees were elective or appointed and most had term limits. It seems in retrospect that every time I was about to end my term there would be a shakeup and the names and titles changed so I would have another three year term with a new committee but doing about the same thing.

The first of these projects was called RMP which stood for Regional Medical Program. Our job as a committee was to sift through grant applications and pick and choose those with enough merit to warrant funding. We would meet fairly regularly in various places, but mostly Portland which was a full day's drive each way for me. It was at these committee functions that I first met some superb individuals that I would cross paths with for many years in multiple capacities. "Dutch" Reinschmidt M.D. was in a leadership role and Dick Grant was a skilled administrator and I would meet them time and time again in roles related to rural health, HSAs (Health Service Areas), and AHEC (Area Health Education Center) functions. Dick was also administrator in various health advisory committees that I served with at the state level.

I did use an airplane, sometimes my own and sometimes commercial if the weather was marginal, for many of the meetings so I would not lose two days travel time out of the office. Many of the projects we reviewed had been pretty well thought out and had some real merit. Some were obviously just wild attempts to get money and had little merit. I was usually not assertive but one project that came up for review stirred me into action. I was a junior member of the committee at the time but one of the few practicing physicians on the committee. The project presented was put forth by a well known and respected VA physician who had done a fair amount of research in diabetes. His proposal was to study the incidence of diabetes and to detect new cases in the migrant farm worker population. His protocol was basically to do mass fasting blood sugars on the migrant farm workers, which seemed like a worthwhile project. His methodology however left me sputtering. He wanted the farm workers to not drink anything or eat breakfast on a specified day during which his team would come to the fields sometime between the hours of eight a.m. and noon and take blood samples. He left no doubt in his presentation that he was an expert in diabetes and that no one should question his protocol. I could not stay quiet and announced to the committee that he might be an expert in diabetes but he certainly was not knowledgeable about his target population. I was much more familiar with his target population than he was. He worked in a VA hospital with chronic and inactive patients who were captive subjects. I pointed out that these field workers would normally be up by three or four a.m., eat a large breakfast, and be in the fields at daybreak about five thirty a.m. By eight or ten in the morning they would already have put in several hours of hard work and would be very hungry and thirsty if they had remained fasting. I convinced the committee that his protocol would not meet the generally accepted criteria usually applied to the term "fasting" (first thing in the morning without anything to eat or drink and before any significant exertion). I also pointed out that after several hours of hard physical labor without food or drink the workers might be suffering other problems. I suggested that he might change his methodology and go to the homes of the workers at four a.m. to take their samples. He made some disparaging comments about small town doctors that didn't set too well with the committee and he didn't get his grant.

Later there was a push from Washington to make changes in health care. A massive network of HSAs (Health Service Areas) was set up. Allegedly they were asking for local input as to what was needed, but in essence they were presenting guidelines to be adopted by decree if the local area committees did not make comments and recommendations within very short and strict timeframes. The logistics of setting up these HSAs was parceled out to the states and regions within the states. I believe the requirements for action were deliberately set in tight timeframes so that the guidelines could be imposed by decree, as they knew that no one could respond quickly enough to challenge them. There was a lot of misinformation, and a lot of deceit by the federal government health planners while these programs were being promoted. Dr. Tanaka, my wonderful associate, was president of the Oregon Medical Association at the time that the National Democratic Party was conducting "fact finding hearings" on health care issues. He was given one and a half minutes to testify after the Welfare Mothers had been given two hours to testify, and the Migrant and Indian Coalition was given one and a half hours. When Dr. Tanaka's time to testify finally came up he was faced with a nasty castigation from Leonard Woodcock (President of the United Auto Workers Union) who was a "citizen" member of the committee. Mr. Woodcock blamed the medical profession for adding a one thousand dollar cost to each automobile to cover the cost of health care for their workers. Senator Ted Kennedy then grandstanded with a political speech hammering organized medicine for not providing quality care for all Americans regardless of their ability to pay. After these two finished their tirades Dr. Tanaka was allowed his ninety seconds to try to explain all that organized medicine was trying to do to improve quality and access to health care. After that grilling Dr. Tanaka was asked to be interviewed on a Portland TV station. He was treated more respectfully in that interview but didn't realize till well into the session that the lady interviewing him was sending hand signals to the cameraman so that much of what he was trying to say was being edited out on the spot. Additional editing before the newscast further took his statements out of context and Dr. Tanaka faced an angry mob of physicians that evening because what they had seen on TV had placed organized medicine in a very bad light. It looked like he had sold the doctors down the river. We in medicine have one agenda and it is to do the best for the patient that we possibly can. We don't comprehend the political agendas of destruction and falsification that are supposed to be acceptable to meet a goal. Furthermore, there is no room for dishonesty in medicine. It is a shame that it is so common in politics and in the press.

Nationwide, the regional HSAs responded with incredible speed and responsibility to thwart a virtual governmental take over. The bureaucracy is used to moving slowly and didn't think that the public could move quickly when challenged. They forgot how rapidly the nation responded to the serious threats we faced in WWII when the movers and shakers of the private sector were able to gear up the war effort in a manor incomprehensible to the entrenched civil servants. As the HSAs were gradually phased out, the states took more responsibility in health planning.

I was appointed to various state committees, with various titles and responsibilities, but all with advisory status. In the 1980s when I served on the Oregon Health Council and on the Public Health Advisory Board, I sensed a potential problem with the delivery of health services under some emergency situations. I had been aware that in much of the 1970s, during periods of rampant inflation, hospitals and other health care providers had stockpiled goods and supplies as much as possible because to buy them later would be more expensive. In the 1980s it made more fiscal sense to adapt to the "supply when needed" concept and count on deliveries to be on a very strict arrival time basis. My suspicion was that any disruption of transportation or electricity could lead to a likely inability to provide services after only a few days. To study this possibility I prepared a questionnaire, under the auspices of the Public Health Division, which was sent to hospitals, emergency services providers, public health officials, and other providers. While I had included some questions which were not well designed, and led to some equivocal answers, in general my suspicions were confirmed that hospital and other emergency medical services would break down within a very short time in the event of transportation disruption or widespread electrical shortages. One example was the surprise expressed by some emergency vehicle services (police, fire, ambulance) when asked how long they could operate their vehicles with electrical outages. When they realized that they could not deliver gasoline to their vehicles or run their pumps, they developed an uneasiness that they had not anticipated. For example, they had not made contingency plans for emergency generators. Food to hospitals and to other food services and grocery stores would suffer severe problems within just a few days. The scenarios presented for consideration could include a nationwide trucker strike as well as ice storms, tornadoes, floods, sabotage, or other man-made or natural disasters.

It does not take a particularly vivid imagination to visualize the escalating chaos which would probably develop if this type of situation lasted for more than just a few days. Those who had not prepared for such disasters, especially those who had become dependent on government for instructions and handouts, would not likely be patient when they were hungry and cold. Law and order would likely break down, looting and other crimes against law abiding citizens would likely escalate, and the situation could rapidly become uncontrollable. We had a small demonstration of this scenario years later in the

148

Hurricane Katrina disaster where looting, rape, and murder compounded the natural disaster.

The Public Health Advisory Board, of which I was a member, was made up of concerned and dedicated citizens and they were quite interested in my project. Much to my dismay the state bureaucracy looked at the project, not with a "what can we do to prepare against such a scenario" attitude, but with the admonition that I had trespassed on another agency's responsibility, and that this study should have been under the auspices of "Emergency Services" rather than the Public Health Division. What I learned about our state government in that exercise was not comforting.

Another frustration I experienced in my role on the Public Health Advisory Board involved our local nursing home. The State Public Health Division had been appointed as the controlling agency for nursing home certification and inspections. One year it appeared that the marching orders from Washington were to clamp down on "abuse" in nursing homes. What qualified as abuse became ridiculous, but it gave the lower level inspection teams great ammunition for penalizing nursing homes nation wide. Our local nursing home provided compassionate care on a shoestring budget and there was no evidence of patient abuse in any common sense interpretation of the word. After one inspection our nursing home was penalized severely for several "patient abuse" infractions. For punishment they had been denied admission of any new Medicare patients (a very significant source of their revenue), they had been fined severely, and had some other restrictions placed on them that I don't recall. I had some patients in the nursing home and I knew that it didn't deserve the punishment they suffered so I took it upon myself to check it out. Some of the infractions were for building maintenance problems such as old paint with some peeling, and other deficiencies of a routine nature. What did catch my eye was the grossly unfair assessment of the patient abuse cases. One obese patient who had an extremely difficult personality had been losing weight. This patient complained about the food and spit out or threw on the floor most of her meals. The doctor who was caring for this lady had spent countless hours trying to pacify her wants, working with dieticians and the family, all to no avail. The inspection team labeled her weight loss to be an abuse problem. That year the national guidelines apparently specified that weight loss in a nursing home was to be classified as abuse, unless it had been documented that there was a justifiable reason.

Another case of "abuse" turned out to be of a patient that had been admitted to the nursing home several years before with severe skin ulcers secondary to a neurological disease. He had been getting very expensive and labor intensive skin care the whole time he was in the nursing home, but the inspection team took his comment that "they don't turn me often enough" to be justification for abuse. That year if any patient had a skin ulcer it was considered abuse. A third case of so-called abuse was that of an elderly deaf lady with a loud voice and a drunken sailor's vocabulary. She had been in the common visitor's area, loudly interrupting those who were visiting other patients. Because she was deaf one of the nursing aides wrote on a piece of paper that she should stop yelling, or she would be taken to her room. That note apparently was proof of a threat, and any threat was considered abuse.

I think there were one or two more minor cases (I don't recall the details) but the cases described here qualified for severe punitive measures because of the "abuse" label. I checked with the nursing home administrator and she helped me get more information. I found in the charts in the record room that all three of these cases had been well documented, and that Dr. Burdic, who had been the doctor in all three, had written quite detailed letters about all of these cases refuting the charges. Copies of these letters, which had been sent to the Public Health Division, were in the patient's charts. I had accumulated a lot of information from the charts and letters and had copies to take to Portland where I planned to present them to the advisory board. One day, a few weeks before the board meeting occurred, Christine Gebbe who was then the Administrator of the Public Health Division happened to be in town and dropped by my office. I showed her the material I had accumulated and she was shocked. She asked where I had gotten the material, including the letters. I answered that all the information was taken from the patient's records in the record room library at the nursing home, and that the inspectors should have looked there before passing judgment. I further informed her that as head of the department she might find it more than a bit embarrassing in a court of law if she had to defend the determination of the term "abuse" as used by her inspectors. To her credit she went through the material in considerable detail and promptly called the person in charge of the nursing home inspections from my office and started action for reversal of the charges. The nursing home had already taken a severe financial hit from loss of revenue but at least the fines were dropped. At the next Public Health Advisory Board meeting there was some discussion of the situation, and there was an apology from the administrator for the errors of the inspection team. Their greatest apology however seemed to be that the letters, which they agreed might have made a difference, had arrived but somehow didn't get to the right person.

After the meeting Christine asked me to visit with the nurse in charge of the nursing home inspections. This lady was a bit defensive and miffed that her rulings had been overturned. We discussed each case and she had to admit that her crew had not adequately reviewed available data. When it came to the lady with the weight loss she tried to convince me that Dr Burdic was only a doctor and wouldn't know anything about food and diets. She preferred not to acknowledge his efforts with dieticians and family or that he personally had spent vast amounts of time with the patient trying to solve the problem. When it came to the patient who was threatened by having to read a note asking her to be quieter or she would be taken to her room, the inspection director tried to convince me that such action really was abuse. I told her that there was really no other way to communicate with the patient other than by a note, and that the nursing home was working with dedicated but low-pay personnel and could not afford to hire psychologists to be their nurses' aides. I further told her that I thought that the aide had done as good a job as could be expected under the circumstances. I then asked her what she would do in the same circumstance. She was a bit flustered and blurted out "Well, they should have a protocol! ---" To which I replied with the first thing that came to my mind, "Bull----!", and the conversation was over. For any reader who thinks a government employee who has the power to shut you down, and who thinks that they can assess a situation 400 miles away better than the person who is actually faced with the problem, I would hope that you will have second thoughts about wishing the government would run the entire health care system.

One time, while I was chairman of the OHC (Oregon Health Council), I had appointed Sylvia Davidson to head up a subcommittee on a particular issue. Sylvia was a concerned citizen who was very active in health related matters, and while we often differed on how to best

151

handle health care delivery we respected each other. She was definitely for more governmental controls on hospitals and doctors than I was, but she was very fair in considering differing opinions. On this occasion when the committee was very busy and finalizing its report she had us meet at her elegant older house in Portland. I was a member of the committee and as she had scheduled it for mid-day. I planned to fly my plane to Portland in the morning and get back home in the evening. The husband of a very fine Ontario lady doctor who was in Ontario at the time wanted to take the trip with me mainly to get some flying experience, so we flew out in the early morning. Both Portland International airport and the Troutdale airport were fogged in but I was able to land at the Hillsboro airport. It took me a bit longer to get to the meeting from Hillsboro so I was a bit late but the meeting was progressing smoothly when I got there. Sylvia had arranged a very nice lunch for us at her house and during the lunch break I was admiring her house and noticed some pictures on the wall of the den. The pictures were of President Truman and his inner circle. When discussing the pictures with Sylvia I found that her husband was in the pictures and he had been high up in the Truman administration. I then asked Sylvia if she knew David Bell who was a major speech writer for President Truman. She responded affirmatively and expressed great admiration for David and asked how I happened to know him. When I told her that he was my cousin on my mother's side my status with her was considerably elevated. David had been in the Marines in WWII and had rapidly become prominent in post war political circles. He had become the major speech writer for President Truman, and later was Director of the Budget in the Kennedy administration before going on to become the executive vice president of the Ford Foundation. After the meeting concluded my friend and I got back to the airport and learned that a major storm had developed over the mountains on my direct route home. We were able to learn enough about the weather pattern that it looked like we could get home by going south via Burns and pick up a very strong tailwind by doing so. Our trip home was much faster, and far safer, by going an extra hundred miles than it would have been by trying to go straight. I had had a good meeting and my friend learned some piloting skills so it was a good day.

Another time consuming committee that I was involved with was the "Certificate of Needs Committee." I was already on the OHC (Oregon Health Council), the last iteration of the governmental Health Planning

Boards that I served, and I concurrently served on the Public Health Advisory committee as a liaison member from the OHC. Because I came from so far away (about 400 miles) they usually accommodated me by arranging back to back meetings so I could serve both functions on one trip away from the office. I served as chairman of the OHC for a couple of years. About this time in the mid 1980s there was an uproar about the costs of new technology and the federal government was trying to get control of medical costs, so they set up a mechanism for review and evaluation to decide who could have what in the way of expensive new technologies. The state agencies would make decisions as to which institutions would be allowed to acquire the new high tech units. When the applicants wished to challenge the verdict, the case was referred to the Certificate of Needs committee which was a subcommittee of the Public Health Advisory Board. We spent long hours and many days going over very lengthy (and very expensive to the applicant) proposals trying to balance costs, geographical considerations, patient needs, types of conditions and emergencies that would utilize the facility, availability of appropriate specialists, transportation issues including emergency situations in bad weather, and estimates of its utilization. Our primary focus at that time was on the new MRI machines and the new kidney stone ultrasound blasters as these were quite new and expensive technologies. Cat Scans (CT) were fairly well established but we still had some involvement with new requests. The alleged goal of our work was to minimize the high cost of these technologies and to prevent hospitals from getting the equipment if it were to be underutilized. The intent of the planners was to have more sharing among hospitals with fewer units in place. The goals sounded noble enough, and a massive regulatory system was organized, and we were to be the referees in the game of health care competition. What the dreamy governmental economists and the MBA bean counters that were making up the rules didn't understand was that the practice of medicine is dynamic. New technologies rapidly go from expensive single use devices to multi use technologies, machines get better, smaller, and cheaper as more uses are found for them, and even more importantly patients do not schedule their car accidents geographically so as to be near an MRI machine when they get their head injuries. We had to sit through days of testimony from competing hospitals, entrepreneurs who wanted to set up mobile units, large medical clinics – all of whom had good reasons to justify their requests. The hours and costs expended by both the regulators, which

153

included our committee, and those wanting to provide the services were staggering. I wonder how many units could have been set up for the costs required in preparing the formal applications.

As my term limits ended on the state boards and committees I found that my volunteer time was switching more to my increasing role in the teaching of medical students and Family Medicine residents from the medical school in Portland.

Boat At Skilak Lake - Kenai Peninsula - Alaska

Post Graduate Education – Teaching and Students

It is important that physicians keep up with advances in medicine. Usually they are pretty much up to date when they finish their training but within about five years there have been some significant changes that they should be aware of. Sometimes the changes relate to new procedures, and sometimes one needs to learn that a previously accepted treatment has been abandoned. Busy doctors have trouble finding enough uninterrupted time to keep fully abreast of the times by reading. Small town doctors find it hard to get away for meetings but going to refresher courses has historically been an important way to try to keep current. I was extremely disappointed with the first post graduate review course that I took at the University of Oregon Medical School (now renamed OHSU for Oregon Health Sciences University). We were having a statewide epidemic of hepatitis at the time and doctors from all over the state were anxious to know if there was anything new in the field. There was a well known and respected researcher at the university who was lecturing. He discussed new findings in laboratory studies but didn't have much new to offer on treatment or management. Doctors from around the state had been coordinating with their public health departments trying to sensibly allocate the limited supplies of gamma globulin which could prevent or modify the disease for those who had been exposed. One of the doctors in the audience asked the speaker if he had any thoughts on how to prioritize the logistics of who should receive the gamma globulin. Almost everyone in the audience knew how much pressure the doctors were experiencing from the public who wanted to get the gamma globulin shots and how hard it was to try to give it only to those who were at the greatest risk. The speaker responded that he thought it was malpractice if you didn't give it to everyone that wanted the shot. There was an immediate groan from the audience. Every doctor on the front lines immediately felt violated because they knew that if they went home and continued to deny gamma globulin on the basis of a best possible evaluation of the risks, they would be sitting ducks should a person denied come down with the disease. If they were to be sued their chance of losing would be very high because the "expert" at the medical school had announced that it was malpractice to not let everyone have gamma globulin who asked for it. The alternative for self protection would have been to give gamma globulin to everyone who was even remotely exposed until the supply ran out.

155

After that no one, not even those in greatest need could be treated. It was a very damaging comment from an "expert" who really had no experience with the stresses placed on doctors in small communities who were facing epidemics and the associated panic of the public.

At that same meeting there was another demonstration of academic misdirection. During a session in which there were discussions of a variety of subjects, a member of the audience asked about a newly reported procedure for the treatment of stomach ulcers. Those in the audience were wanting to know what the procedure was, who was experienced with the procedure, what were the indications to consider for using the new procedure, etc. They wanted to know who was available for referrals in cases that were appropriate for the procedure. Instead of getting the information they were looking for they were told, "Well, if you were specialists we would tell you." This was a severe slap in the faces of the conscientious doctors who were in the front lines. I doubt that anyone in the room wanted to perform the procedure, but they all felt that they should be aware of its merits and how to refer for specialty care when indicated. Because of the attitude "on the hill" I went elsewhere for quite a few years for my continuing education. Colorado and several other institutions were doing a good job of helping their doctors keep current.

Fortunately in Oregon we had some very dynamic and visionary individuals who did a magnificent job of changing attitudes and improving the system. It didn't happen over night, and I don't remember the exact timelines but I do recall the general sequence. "Dutch" Reinschmidt, who I had worked with at RMP and Rural Health meetings, took on an official role at the medical school dealing with post-graduate education. Dutch had been in private practice and fully understood the difficulties encountered in trying to keep up. He started a program called the "Circuit Course" in which professors and instructors from the medical school would tour the state giving lectures and interacting with local physicians. This allowed the local physicians to get continuing education without having to leave their own towns, and without having to expend a couple of days of travel time. Another great benefit from the circuit courses was that the professors and instructors from the medical school found out, many for the first time, that many of the LMDs ("local medical doctors" – a rather disparaging term often used at the medical school) were actually very competent and dedicated. I think that this program was the greatest single reason for improved relationships between the medical school and the small town doctors around the state.

Another major factor that came in to play which improved the relationship between practicing physicians and OHSU was the formation of the Department of Family Medicine. (I discuss the evolution of the specialty of Family Medicine in another chapter.) As the specialty was being developed schools around the country were gearing up to provide the training necessary to qualify their students for the new specialty. Dr. Laurel Case came on board at OHSU to become the chairman of the new department. He had been in private practice and knew what his students would be facing as they started caring for patients in small towns. He also knew that at the medical school the students would not have a realistic picture of small town practice so he started an elective program designed so that students could go out to small towns and stay with practicing physicians for a few weeks. He organized several general practitioners from all over the state, mostly doctors who had met the requirements for the new specialty of Family Medicine, and worked out some basic guidelines. He arranged for formal university status as Clinical Instructors. Also included was some university insurance to cover the students and us, the preceptors, during the time the students were with us. In the beginning the program was purely elective and those medical students who were interested had to work out a schedule that did not interfere with their required classes. At first I only got a few students per year, but I'm sure that doctors closer to Portland got more students. Over the next twenty plus years that I remained in active practice there was a steady stream of students and family practice residents. The program changed over the years as it evolved from a strictly elective to a required rotation and it became no longer feasible for all of the students to stay in the doctors' homes and live with their families. This increase in housing and scheduling logistics was part of the reason the AHEC (Area Health Education Centers) and NEOAHEC (North East Oregon Health Education Center) programs were developed.

During the early years of the preceptor program we had some great experiences. The students were absolutely wonderful. They were bright and eager. We enjoyed having them live in our house and in several cases they brought their spouses and children. I did not spare them night calls as they were to get full exposure to small town practice. In most cases they were energized by the experience, but in a

157

few cases they decided that they were not up to a general practice schedule and decided to go into pathology or radiology where they would have better control of their hours.

I was absolutely committed to providing the visiting students with a good learning experience and also expose them to the advantages of small town living. I also tried very hard to arrange at least one day of recreation so that they did not get the impression that there is no chance of a break while being a family physician. I knew that during their early exposure to clinical medicine, the stage in their training that they were in at the time, the students usually saw patients that had chronic diseases and had charts that were huge and filled with vast amounts of information. I was convinced that I could provide them with the excitement and challenges of brand new problems. The students were with me on almost every patient visit. If my patient was presenting with a new problem I would frequently, after obtaining permission from the patient, let the student spend 20-30 minutes alone with the patient followed by a discussion of the history and findings and then we would outline a proposed course of treatment. In many cases this was the first time that the students had encountered a brand new problem and they became excited. I don't want to spend a lot of time on case studies but a few learning experiences stand out and are worthy of mention. One of my very early students was Judd Lunn. Judd was a wonderful person. He reminded me of the stereotypical blue-eyed blond, Eagle Scout that we used to see on the cover of *Boys Life*, the scouting magazine that I remember reading during my childhood. Early in Judd's time with me we went into an examining room to see a new patient. We encountered a mother and her teen age daughter and both seemed very apprehensive. I had not seen the girl or her family previously so this was a completely new case. I asked a few questions and immediately realized that this would be a tremendous student learning situation. I had learned in just a few brief words that the teen age girl had developed a severe headache and some visual disturbances for the first time. Rather than point the way for the rest of the interview and examination I explained to the patient and her mother that I would like my student to spend considerable time doing a work up after which we would then get together and make plans for further studies. This was acceptable to them and as I was leaving the room I whispered to the mother that I felt fairly sure that I knew what the problem was but that we needed to do several things to be sure, and I indicated that I didn't think it was going to be terribly serious.

Judd had not seen a lot of patients in the clinics but he had received physical diagnosis training so I felt that he would be able to make a reasonable assessment, and I knew that he would have an outstanding experience. I instructed Judd to take a detailed history and to do a comprehensive neurological examination – at least the best he could with his limited experience. After a half hour or so I brought Judd into the office for a discussion. He understandably had a variety of diagnoses, including brain tumors, to present as possibilities. I realized that he was struggling and had not considered the most likely diagnosis so I asked him to spend some time with text books in the office and to particularly study about migraine headaches. We then returned to the patient and her mother and outlined a treatment program and a set of tests. A patient's first migraine headache with associated temporary blindness is an absolutely terrifying experience, and Judd had been able to be the first on the scene. Many years later Judd, who was an anesthesiologist practicing in Boise, stopped by the office one day while he was traveling through Ontario. It was great to see him and I casually asked him what he knew about migraine headaches. He grinned and seemed surprised that I had recalled the incident but admitted that that episode in my office years previously was one of the greatest learning experiences of his entire medical training. A few years after that visit Judd and his newly graduated dentist son were tragically killed in a small airplane accident – what a loss.

Another of my early students who stood out was Dave Grube. Dave was one of those rare persons that radiate an aura of genuine compassion and gentleness. He was struggling with goals and seemed to find some direction while in Ontario. He became a beloved family doctor in Philomath, Oregon, president of the Oregon Academy of Family Physicians in 1990, member and chairman of the Oregon Board of Medical Examiners, and Oregon Family Doctor of the Year in 1986. He has publicly credited me for inspiring him into family medicine. His written tribute to me is reprinted with permission from the Oregon Academy of Family Physicians and can be found in another chapter. I still get wet eyes whenever I read his beautiful tribute.

Dave on "Office Break"

As the preceptor program increased from a voluntary program to a required rotation for medical students it was becoming very apparent that training off campus had some real merit. We continued to get excellent support from the Family Practice Department as these preceptor programs continued and expanded over the years. When Dr. Case retired the department was led by Dr. Bob Taylor and then by Dr. John Saultz, both of whom have proven to be high quality leaders.

The Family Practice residents were added to the program and then some other medicine related support programs such as physiotherapy also became involved. To accommodate all this new activity more doctors and other training personnel were required and new arrangements for housing needed to be developed. Again Dutch Reinschmidt and Dick Grant were instrumental in organizing and obtaining funding for AHEC programs to help with the needed logistics. Several smaller areas in the state were identified for local area programs. As the needs were identified and funding was acquired, the local areas needed to organize. I was appointed to a steering committee to help set up NEOAHEC. Our job was basically to set goals, write bylaws, and pick a director. We had several applicants for the director's job and we agonized through the process of choosing. When we got down to the last few applicants we were becoming rather discouraged. Some applicants had pretty good resumés but didn't meet expectations at interview, one applicant apparently had falsified some information, and one with lots of experience in writing grants appeared not to have any vision of what could be done with the organization. Our last applicant had very little experience with what would normally have been the expected background. She had run a local computer business and had some other business and educational experience but at interview she blossomed with ideas and a vision that literally blew us away. A day that looked pretty dismal suddenly was energized. We immediately chose Sandy Ryman as our director and she has remained an excellent choice for many years. After the steering committee's job was done I spent several years on the Board of Directors. NOAHEC has had a big job coordinating schedules with the medical school, obtaining housing, doing outreach to high school students encouraging them to enter health-related occupations, and finding private funding as federal funding dried up.

I continued to work with medical students and family practice residents until I retired from active practice in 1994. After I closed my office I did some *locum tenens* work, filling in for doctors in Oregon and Washington. I also spent some time teaching at the Family Practice Residency program in Klamath Falls, a satellite program of the OHSU family medicine department. When I retired I was advanced to the title of Clinical Professor Emeritus in the Department of Family Medicine. I probably could win a prize for being the professor who spent the least amount of time on campus and still rose to full professorship. My only time on campus was for departmental training sessions and refresher courses. I never had an office on campus and never taught in the department clinics.

Doctor D at Office Desk Circ. 1990

Eastern Oregon Corral

Jim's Landing - Skilak Lake - Kenai Peninsula - Alaska

Retirement

When I closed my office in 1994 it was with very mixed emotions. We had simplified the process by previously having our group sell the clinic building to the hospital and becoming renters. I was able to negotiate with the hospital to purchase much of my medical equipment and supplies so I didn't have to have an auction or deal with equipment supply houses. The hope was that having an already equipped office ready to occupy would make the process of recruiting a new physician somewhat easier. I had really hoped to hold on for the arrival of Paul Gehring who had spent some time with me both officially and unofficially while he was a medical student at OHSU in Portland. It would have been nice to have had him just take over my practice but it would have been a couple of years before he would be available. Toddy was adamant that we not wait that long as she wanted to do some "retirement stuff" before her health deteriorated further. By this time she was having frequent bouts of chest pain resulting in multiple emergency room visits, echocardiograms, and cardiac catheterizations so she knew she was likely to become more disabled as time went on.

It is a given that if you are in private practice and paying for your own employees salaries and benefits, plus supplies, fees, insurance and licenses, you are going to have to work pretty much full time and at full bore just to pay the overhead. That scenario does not allow a person in private practice to phase down and take more time off to ease into retirement. I arranged to do some work for a local urgent care clinic after I closed the office and that gave me some income without any overhead expenses. Also I had arranged to work for a *Locum Tenens* company which contracted with physicians like me to fill in for doctors who needed some time off for education or vacation. This arrangement allowed my wife and me the opportunity to have expense paid trips to different communities and allowed us to explore new geographic areas. For the first time in my medical career I was expected to keep regular hours and was seldom required to cover night calls. I really had a difficult time adjusting to a normal work week, but it was great for my wife as she could pretty much predict, for the first time in many years, when I would be home. On these jaunts I usually had a day or two of off time which allowed us to explore the area. On one locums assignment I was covering a clinic in Odessa, Washington and we got to tour the fabulous geologic formations related to the ice age catastrophic floods which created the scablands. The story of those floods and the explanation of how they formed the scablands are well worth studying. I spent some time at clinics in Pullman, Washington and Lakeview, Oregon. I also spent some time teaching at the Klamath Falls, Oregon, Family Practice Residency program which was affiliated with the Family Medicine Department at OHSU in Portland.

On one of my stints helping out at Lakeview I was working with Bob Bomengen while his partner was taking some time off. Bob had been starting down a surgical and orthopedic residency path when he decided that he really wanted to be a small town doctor and he gave up an offer of an orthopedic residency and moved to Lakeview. In his practice he had many incredible emergencies to deal with and his surgical training was put to the test on many occasions. Lakeview is one of the most isolated communities in Oregon and in bad weather all forms of transportation can be shut down. Bob would on occasion fly difficult problem cases to Portland in his own plane or utilize a local volunteer air ambulance service to transport critical patients if the weather would allow and if the patient was stable enough for transport. There were times, however, where circumstances were such that he had to dive in and do what he could with what he had, unable to get any help. One such incident involved an accidental gunshot wound in a young man who was suffering massive blood loss and whose only chance of survival required immediate surgery and multiple transfusions. Bob dove into a very difficult surgical problem and he mobilized the town to get walking blood donors because the standard blood supply was quickly overwhelmed. This story in considerable detail was written up in the *Readers Digest*. Bob became the Oregon Family Doctor of the Year and then he was named the National Family Doctor of the Year in 1994. He is the only Oregon physician to be so named. His type of isolated community with its extra demands has been called "Frontier Medicine" rather than just Family Medicine.

One morning I was assisting Bob in surgery. Everything was going smoothly and Bob casually starting talking to the operating crew. His comments were something like this, "I want all of you people to know that the man standing across the table from me, Dr. Daniels, is the reason I am here in Lakeview." I was flabbergasted because I had known a little bit about Bob but had not known him well and didn't have a clue about his claim. I sputtered a bit and asked him what he was referring to. His response was, "Do you remember one evening

164

years ago when you flew from Ontario to Portland to talk to a bunch of medical students about being a family doctor in a small town?" Yes, I had recalled that evening. Bob went on to explain to me and the operating crew that he was one of the students that I had talked to that evening and he was so impressed about my Alaska stories as well as stories from my early practice in Eastern Oregon that he had said to himself "I want to become a family doctor just like Dr. Daniels." Wow! - Another totally unexpected tribute that caught me totally by surprise. Actually, while I may have nudged him a bit towards family medicine I think his wife had a lot more influence on where he settled than I did – she had been brought up in Lakeview.

I was scheduled again to spend several weeks instructing at the Family Practice Residency Program at Klamath Falls when I developed another excruciatingly painful ruptured disk in my low back. I was forced to cancel that trip and underwent another one of my multiple back surgeries. (I've lost count but I think I have had 14 or 15 back and neck surgeries.) By the time I had recovered from that operation it was apparent that Toddy was having enough medical problems that we really couldn't plan very far ahead so it made sense to fully retire from the practice of medicine.

One of the retirement activities that Toddy and I really enjoyed was the Elderhostel program. These educational programs for senior citizens were available all over the world and involved many subjects. The choices of programs were extremely varied and involved classroom study, workshops and field trips. The organization is non-profit and as reasonably priced as could be expected. Some of the classes we took were about photography which had been one of my main life long hobbies. (I had started taking pictures as a child of perhaps eight or nine years of age. By early high school my brother had instructed me in darkroom techniques of developing film, enlarging, dodging and burning.) One Elderhostel photographic program was at Marble Canyon near the upper end of the Grand Canyon (see color photo) and another involved being on one of four houseboats on Lake Powell for a week. The houseboats were full so we got to be pretty cozy with strangers. Everyone had a great time. Our photography instructor on both of those trips was Gary Ladd who has been widely published in *Arizona Highways* and several other publications. He knew the country well and knew when the light would be best at different locations. He gave lectures on the geology of the area as well as great tips on photo techniques. There were other instructors at these courses who lectured on the history of the area. Other Elderhostel trips that we took were about Arizona wildlife, plants and mining history – all with interesting instructors from area colleges. One of our early courses was at Gatlinburg, Tennessee, not far from Toddy's childhood home. We spent two weeks taking one week each on learning to make pottery and stained glass. It was pretty apparent by the time the classes were over that I had best spend my time on photography rather than pottery or stained glass but we learned a lot and had lots of fun.

Our youngest child, De Wilda, had been struggling with medical and personal problems for many years and we had helped her obtain and upgrade a log cabin in the Montana mountains west of Missoula. Toddy and I enjoyed relaxing in the mountains and helping De Wilda as much as we could with our own limitations. By this time in the early 2000s Toddy was requiring supplemental oxygen much of the time and I had rigged up an oxygen system for traveling in our Conversion Van. I had purchased a refurbished oxygen concentrator and powered it for travel with a high capacity inverter which kept it going while we were traveling. We couldn't park very long on our travels because of the drain on the battery so we had to keep moving until we could plug into 110 Volt A.C. Emergency oxygen tanks for intermittent use had been previously satisfactory but they didn't last long and getting them filled while traveling, especially to remote areas, was difficult. On our last trip to Montana while Toddy was still alive I left her in the care of our daughter so that I could attend a conference with my son Don. I was at his house in Evergreen, Colorado preparing to leave for a fun UFO conference when I got a call that Toddy had been rushed to the Missoula hospital with another episode of severe chest pain. I abandoned my trip plans and flew to Missoula. Tests did not show any cardiac muscle damage at that time so she left the hospital and again refused to take prescribed medications. Toddy had read a lot about "adverse reactions" and refused many medications that might have helped her. She also had developed periods of irrational behavior. She remained alert most of the time but could suddenly fly into an abusive rage for no apparent reason. Whether this was partially a drug reaction or perhaps cerebral hypoxia was never known. I have great admiration for the cardiologists and cardiac surgeons who patiently did so much for her under trying circumstances. In her last few years she had many cardiac catheterizations with angioplasty. Her diseased mitral valve deteriorated so much that she required a valve replacement and at the same surgery she had coronary bypass procedures.

I have great empathy for caregivers, usually the spouses, who deal with day-to-day stresses and uncertainties of severe illness of any kind in a family member. I don't think that most people fully appreciate the constant stress those caregivers experience. My blood pressure rose, I didn't sleep well, I couldn't go anywhere without being in constant communication. Fortunately my son Alan and his wife Linda lived nearby and were of great help. They kept reassuring me that the frequent verbal abuse we were all experiencing was part of the illness and we should try to accept the fact that she was not herself. Her final terminal episode was not directly a heart problem but was related to her long term vascular disease. I was returning from a conference I had attended in Boise, Idaho and pulled into the driveway just as she was being loaded into an ambulance. She had developed sudden abdominal pain and diarrhea. Emergency evaluation at Holy Rosary Medical Center suggested an abdominal vascular catastrophe and she was helicoptered by Life Flight to Boise to be met by vascular surgeons who took her immediately into surgery. By the time I got to the Boise hospital by car the surgeons had already found an occlusion of the superior mesenteric artery due to an embolus. They did what they could but the bowel could not recover and she passed away in less than twenty four hours on July 23, 2003. She had requested that there be no services and that she be cremated. Many months later when our friend Clint Bellows was visiting the area he helped me complete the last of her requests – namely to scatter her ashes in the campground and wilderness areas that we all loved so much. The picture in the color section shows a favorite rock in one of our favorite camping areas. In the picture is my entire family as it was in 1987, all gathered on the rock. We referred to ourselves as the "Daniels Rock Group." That is where some of her ashes are scattered. The rest we scattered up the trail toward some of our favorite hiking destinations.

In the first several months after Toddy died I had a lot of work to do catching up on projects that had been put on hold. The yard needed a lot of attention and while I enjoyed yard work I was finding that my multiple back problems had slowed me down and my physical productivity was definitely diminished. In September of that year my daughter-in-law Linda decided that I needed to start mixing more with

167

people and she set up a well-advertised birthday party for me on the lawn of my house. There was a large turnout of friends, relatives, colleagues, nurses, and patients from as far away as Utah and Colorado. As I think about those that attended my party I am surprised at the large numbers who have since passed away.

One who attended the birthday party was a lady that I had known slightly for many years. Maxine had had a difficult childhood and started working at a very young age. She had, by guts and determination, bettered herself and had taken training as a respiratory therapist, then starting our RT department at Holy Rosary Hospital. She had raised five children with marginal help from her husbands. She studied for the difficult Nursing Home Administrators exams and became the administrator of our local nursing home. She had fairly recently lost her husband to a long and difficult Alzheimer's illness. We were both suffering from what I call "caregivers fatigue", and we both enjoyed each other's companionship. We tried a marriage but it just didn't work out and only lasted about a year.

I did some traveling to visit my sister Mino in McMinnville, Oregon a few times. Not long after Toddy died I went to see Don and his family in Evergreen, Colorado. It had been quite a few years since I had flown as pilot but Don, who is a United Airlines pilot, wanted to give me a bit of excitement. He arranged for me to fly the United Airlines 757 simulator at the United Airlines Training Center in Denver. Those simulators are fantastic with their ability to produce a realistic picture on a screen that you quickly substitute in your mind for the real terrain and airport. The instructor took me through several approaches to the airport and set me up to land the plane myself. The plane tilts and vibrates and you hear and feel the thump as the landing gear come down. I flared at the right time and made a slightly rough landing but the instructor assured me that I didn't kill anybody. That was a great experience. I took a couple of trips to New Mexico to visit Clint and Sal Bellows. In 2005 Don arranged for me to go to Shanghai on his Boeing 777. His wife Terry and I spent a few days sight-seeing even though Don had to return with his plane the day after we arrived. Terry and I had a great time but you don't get to see much of China in three days. I did get some interesting pictures. I spent a few weeks in Alaska in 2006 while my son Alan was working at a fish processing plant in Kenai during the salmon run. He was very busy so I took some very productive photo expeditions on my own. In 2007 Alan and I were able to get to the family cabin in Wisconsin. I had not been there for about ten years and he had not been able to get there for more than thirty years. In 2008 Alan, Linda, and I were able to get to the cabin again and were able to take in the EAA (Experimental Aircraft Association) annual meetings at Oshkosh, Wisconsin.

I was able to sell my big house that we built in 1965 to Tom and Bonnie Russell who wanted to get out of California, and they have put in a lot of work to upgrade the property. I then moved in to a new manufactured home on Alan and Linda's property where they spoil me royally and feed me almost every evening.

I have continued to spend considerable time with my hobby of photography and I have recently been appointed to chair a committee of the Malheur Country Historical Society with the assignment of upgrading and reprinting a two volume set of books on local history that had previously been printed in 1988. I have been busy writing this book which started out as "a few stories for my grandkids." My grandkids now have provided me with eight of the most wonderful great-grand-children a person could ever hope for. I am so proud of my grandchildren who are proving themselves to be very worthy parents. I only hope that my grand-children and great-grandchildren can grow up in a country that has as much to offer as we experienced.

Katie holding Matthew, Ami, Dorin, Rachel, Emily, Tony,- 2007 - Two more Great-Grandchildren Since

Malheur Butte - Ontario, Oregon

Skilak Lake - Near Kenai, Alaska

Oops, Close Calls, and Missed Headlines

I have often heard it said that a grown boy is a miracle. As we grow older and watch our own children, grandchildren, and great-grandchildren grow up we realize more and more the truth of this statement. Most of us tend to have an attitude of indestructibility, even with the knowledge that bad things happen – we think they just happen to other people. While I pondered this bit of philosophy I started to recall some brief incidents in my life that could have turned out very differently had there been just a tiny displacement in distance, time, or situation. Fortunately we generally don't dwell on these situations or we could be so paralyzed with self preservation fears that we would accomplish nothing.

When I was in the 6 to 12 year age group I had a few close calls that could have seriously impacted my life.

One time while using our tiny bathroom on the first floor in our Madison house I casually reached over to pull the metal light chain while still touching a faucet with the other hand. We probably still had the original 1921 electrical wiring. I instantly became a piece of sixty cycle vibrating protoplasm. It seemed like an eternity before I was able to let go, even though it was probably only twenty or thirty seconds. "PROFESSOR'S SON FOUND DEAD IN BATHROOM – ELECTROCUTION SUSPECTED" -----Nope – not this time.

As a child living in Madison there were many places to swim in the multiple lakes. Most kids were placed in some sort of swimming lessons so they could handle themselves in water. One of the times when I was fooling around during swimming lessons I dove into shallow water. My neck hurt for awhile but in those days you didn't go to a doctor for "minor things." Years later a two view chest x-ray showed a wedged cervical vertebra leading to the conclusion that I had suffered a compression fracture of my neck sometime in the past. "BOY BREAKS NECK WHILE DIVING – NOW PARAPLEGIC" ---- Not this time either.

I was probably about seven or eight years old when my brother and I were exploring the high bluffs on the Green Bay side of Door County in Wisconsin. We were crawling through dense brush and I was not being too observant when I suddenly felt my brother grab my leg and yell at me just as I was about to go over a 200 foot precipice. ----

"BOY FALLS TO HIS DEATH OFF CLIFF- BROTHER UNABLE TO STOP HIM IN TIME" – Nope – no headlines this time either.

One time at our cabin a bunch of kids from along the beach took a hike up the highway to explore the small dam at the bottom of Kangaroo Lake. The others were walking and accompanied by the mother of one of the boys. I was the only one riding a bike. The highway was a narrow two lane highway and I was fooling around going ahead on my bike and circling back to join the others. I was riding slowly and as I made one of my slow circles I was just about on the centerline of the highway and became unbalanced and started to tip over just as a car went by "going like sixty." (In those days sixty miles an hour was extremely fast - hence the term "going like sixty") The car didn't miss me by more than a foot or so and I can still remember the scream from the mother who was with us. ----"BOY RIDING BIKE FALLS IN FRONT OF SPEEDING CAR – INSTANTLY KILLED" Not this time either – no headlines.

My father went with me when I took the driving exam for my driver's license. While I was taking the exam I was timid but doing OK and the inspector asked me to turn right at the next street. As I turned onto the narrow street I was suddenly, and totally unexpectedly, confronted by a city bus that swerved into my lane of traffic totally blocking the entire street. I don't think I would have been seriously injured but it might have been a pretty good "ouch" (remember – we didn't have seat belts then and fairly low impact collisions could have fairly severe consequences). Somehow I was able to duck into an unoccupied driveway and avoided a collision. The inspector turned pale and after a few minutes told me to go back to the office. I didn't know what he had in mind because I thought there was more examining to be done. When we got back to the office my dad was waiting and he cheerfully asked the inspector if I had passed - to which the inspector replied "Y-y-y-e-e-e-s-s-s!" He was still pale and shaking. I got my license and there were no headlines. "TEEN AGE BOY CRASHES INTO BUS WHILE TAKING DRIVER LICENSE EXAM - EXAMINER INSISTS BUS DRIVER AT FAULT" - It might have been an interesting story.

When I was in college a few of my friends and I drove to the family cabin in Door County, Wisconsin for a weekend vacation. We probably had a few beers but none of us drank heavily and we didn't drink before driving home so the events to follow were not alcohol related. As I was driving home (about a two hundred mile trip) we were visiting and I was not very attentive. As I approached the top of a hill on a curving road I wandered over the center line just as another car came over the hill. One of my friends saw the oncoming car before I did and he grabbed the steering wheel and jerked it just in time to avoid a head on collision. "COLLEGE BOYS KILLED IN HEAD-ON CRASH" – Close, but no headlines.

In a previous chapter I mentioned how a plane crashed into my greenhouse while I was doing research at Eniwetok. Had I not been late doing my work in the greenhouse because of being diverted by reading a classified document I would have been a direct hit. "OAK RIDGE SCIENTIST KILLED BY FALLING AIRPLANE WHILE WATERING HIS PLANTS" - that story would need a bit of explanation. I was about six feet away instead of ground zero by mere happenstance.

A couple of other airplane related incidents occurred with Cessna 195 airplanes that I owned. When I bought my first 195 I was informed that they were great planes but had two nasty characteristics. The big radial engines had a tendency to catch fire – but not to worry – just keep cranking till the engine starts and it will suck out the fire. The other problem was that being a short coupled tail dragger it had a tendency to ground loop. Well, while on a trip in the first 195 we had stopped to visit my sister in Kansas. We loaded up the next morning and when I tried to start the engine it caught fire. I kept cranking while my wife was throwing the kids and luggage out on the tarmac. She was screaming at me to get out but I kept trying to get the engine to start. My brother in-law had taken us to the airport and he called the fire department and we promptly had help but the airplane was badly damaged. Had the gas in the wings over my head caught fire I would have sizzled. "ONTARIO DOCTOR BURNS UP IN AIRPLANE FIRE" – It didn't seem too serious at first but it could have been bad.

The other Cessna 195 situation could also have turned out differently. On a flight from Ontario to Wisconsin in my second 195 we had landed for gas and food in South Dakota before heading on to Door County. It was then after dark and we were deviating from our intended route to get around thunder storms when my oldest boy Don tapped me on the knee and pointed to the oil pressure gauge that was slowly falling. It was dark, I knew which direction I was from a VOR station but not exactly how far I was (in those days the radio navigation equipment was not nearly as sophisticated as it is now) so I really didn't know where the nearest airport was located. I got on the radio with Green Bay Flight Service Station asking for help. From the information I was able to give them they thought I was probably near Oshkosh and about that same time my wife spotted an airport beacon which we headed for immediately. I had slowed the plane down to make it as easy on the engine as possible – I was concerned that the engine would freeze up and quit if we ran completely out of oil. We didn't have the radar coverage then that we have now so the FAA couldn't pinpoint my position and guide me in. As I approached the airport (it was Oshkosh) I lined up for a downwind landing because I knew I could make it to that runway, but if the engine quit I wasn't sure I could make it around the field to the preferred runway. The landing I made was good and as I was rolling along I tapped on the brakes to slow down for a turnoff and one brake worked and the other didn't so we immediately went into a ground loop which tipped us up on one wingtip, bent one landing gear, and closed the active runway. In flying if you make it to the runway and walk away from the plane it is a "good" landing. This one was a "good" landing that was hard on the ego as well as the pocket book. The irony of the situation was that I had arranged for a mechanic to check the oil lines and the brakes before this trip and both systems had failed. The ground loop was not headline worthy but the chance of an engine quitting at night over unknown territory was potentially very bad. "DOCTOR AND FAMILY LOST IN PLANE – HAD DECLARED EMERGENCY - LAST RADIO CONTACT AT 9:45 PM. WRECKAGE NOT FOUND – POSSIBLY IN LAKE" I'm really glad that this headline never occurred as the whole family was at risk.

When I had only been in practice a few years I developed a chronic cough. I had smoked since being in the Navy and had only recently quit smoking. I had an x-ray taken at the hospital in Ontario and was called to the radiology area by the visiting radiologist who told me that the x-ray showed carcinoma. He hedged a little bit saying that it was remotely possible that the findings could be from viral pneumonia. This news was devastating to me as I was far from being out of debt and had a young family. Adding to my concern was the fact that my wife and I had strong differences of opinion about life insurance. I felt that a professional man with small children should have life insurance

174

in case anything happened to him so the family could go on. My wife, who had a strong mind of her own, was totally against spending money on life insurance, having been convinced by her father's comments that life insurance was not a good investment. He was a professor of accounting and was old enough and had invested well enough that he had a different perspective than I did. Fortunately the viral pneumonia cleared and I had dodged another bullet. "YOUNG PHYSICIAN DIES OF LUNG CANCER – FAMILY DESTITUTE" – Almost --This episode probably caused me more grief than any other because of the effect it would have had on my young family.

I was probably in my late 40's when I was using a handyman jack while working on a heavy vehicle. I had the vehicle held up by the jack when suddenly there was a click and a swoosh and the jack handle flashed by very close to my head. I think that metal jack handle had enough force and speed to have easily inflicted a fatal blow and it only missed my head by a couple of inches. -- "LOCAL PHYSICIAN KILLED BY JACK HANDLE WHILE WORKING ON VEHICLE" -- Another very close call that just missed by inches. Still no headlines.

I was probably in my early sixties when I needed neck surgery. I was having very distressing nerve compression symptoms in my arm and underwent a cervical spine decompression surgery. Post-op I was doing well until the middle of the night when apparently a vessel came loose and my airway was severely compromised. I called for the nurse and tried to tell her that I was choking. Somehow she didn't understand what I was trying to tell her and she apparently interpreted my complaints as more like gagging instead of choking. I felt myself fading and realized that if I allowed myself to go to sleep I would probably not wake up. I finally convinced the nurse to check my oxygen saturation and it was very low. She then realized that I was in trouble, and once I was given some oxygen I started to stabilize. When Dr. Henbest checked me he was very concerned as I had developed a massive hematoma which was compressing my airway. He was about to take me back into surgery but I seemed to be stabilizing and gradually improved. I needed oxygen for about a week at home until I could breathe normally. I felt sorry for Dr. Henbest as he had planned to take a wonderful trip with the Fish and Game officials to tag sturgeon. He had been planning the trip for months but he wouldn't leave while I was in distress. He refused to turn me over to someone else. This was definitely a life threatening complication. -- "DOCTOR

DIES FROM COMPLICATIONS OF SURGERY" -- This was an awfully close call but I continued to avoid the headlines.

At my age of 81 I am not looking for more close calls to record – I am old enough now that most anything would be considered "natural causes."

Honors, Awards, and Titles

The only titles or awards that I actively pursued were the M.D. degree and the Board Certification for the specialty of Family Medicine. Those were necessary pursuits that allowed me to be licensed and to do what I had always wanted to do. As time went on I seemed to get all sorts of awards and titles that I had not sought. Titles actually meant very little to me and I was happy to just be "Doc." I was honored with several student-promoted awards for my teaching activities, and because of my affiliation with the University (OHSU) I was given the title of Clinical Instructor. After many years of serving as an Instructor I was visited one day by a team from the Family Medicine Department who came on a survey trip. After watching my office in action they went into a huddle and confronted me with profuse apologies because they suddenly realized that I had been working for years as a Clinical Instructor and most other doctors in the program had been elevated to Associate or Assistant Clinical Professor. In the academic setting the advancement in title appears to be extremely important and usually carries with it advancement in pay. As I, along with the other preceptors in the program, was serving as a volunteer without pay, the lack of advancement in title didn't bother me a bit. I was surprised to have been so profusely apologized to for something I hadn't been concerned about. After that visit I was rapidly elevated through the steps of professorship and when I retired I was elevated to full "Clinical Professor Emeritus." I received plaques and certificates for my services in health planning, public health, and rural health. One very nice award that I received caught me completely by surprise. Unbeknownst to me I was picked to be the Family Doctor of the Year for the State of Oregon in 1983. I was sitting at a luncheon table at the annual OAFP (Oregon Academy of Family Physicians) meetings at Salishan, a resort on the Oregon coast, and listening to some nice talk about the doctor who was receiving the award for the year. A few testimonials were read and some taped interviews were played before I realized that they were talking about ME! My family knew this was coming but I didn't have a clue. What a surprise! Of all the nice honors I received the one that I cherish the most and which still makes me choke up every time I read it is the beautiful tribute written by Dr. David Grube, one of my very early students. It is published here with permission from the Oregon Academy of Family Physicians.

Finding My Hero in Ontario
By David Grube MD

  In 1971, as a third year medical student, I was still uncertain about my future plans as a physician. The "specialty" of family medicine was early in its evolution, and I was not encouraged, at the University of Oregon Medical School (now OHSU), to seek this path, in fact, quite the contrary. General/family physicians were condescendingly referred to as "LMDs" (local medical doctors). I distinctly remember my internal medicine resident wondering "why on earth anyone would want to be a doctor in a small town." But I had met Laurel Case, a new faculty member, and he had set up a novel preceptorship program, and I had been assigned to spend two weeks with Dorin Daniels in Ontario, Oregon.

  For all young American men those were disturbing years. My peers were being drafted and sent to Southeast Asia to fight in a war many of us couldn't understand, and many of us didn't believe in. A few months earlier we listened to the radio in histology lab as we were given a "lottery" (sic) number for the military draft, which randomly and radically changed each of our futures and hence each of our potentials.

  So, I found myself driving my Ford Pinto east to a frontier town I had never heard of, to a part of Oregon I had never seen. In my first two years at the medical school I had not found my educational experience to have been inspiring or even very stimulating.

  But before I left Portland, surprisingly, I had received a letter from Dr. Daniels. In it he welcomed me, he asked what he could do to make my experience with him successful, and he wrote "I would like to know what your particular recreational interests might be so at least a small amount of fun can be programmed into your stay." I didn't know what to expect, but I thought I knew that this was going to be a great experience. I thought I knew, but I didn't.

  Dorin Daniels had been practicing in eastern Oregon since 1958. Under Dr. Case's new program, Dr. Daniels had taught only a few medical students prior to my arrival. But he was a well established LMD, and in my first few hours I quickly learned that he was not only respected and admired by his patients, the nursing staff, and his peers, but that he was extremely competent, very thorough, and compassionate in ways that I had rarely seen demonstrated by physicians I knew. But most of all, HE LOVED WHAT HE WAS DOING!

Dr. Daniels wasted no time incorporating me into his practice and into his day. He had a busy schedule that few of us today could imagine, and that few of us could abide, but his style was to include me into everything that he did (asking me, teaching me, using me, helping me) as he cared for a wide variety of folk of all ages. We got up early, (his wife, Toddy, had welcomed me into their home) and made house calls on the way to the hospital to make rounds. In the clinic we saw an endless stream of patients, all of whom he knew personally, most of whom were members of families he cared for as well. He seemed to be energized by each of them - their needs strengthened his service. He and Toddy unselfishly shared their home, their work, and their family play with me - their energy was extraordinary.

He taught me the basics: Touch every patient. The patient is the one with the disease. Nurture the nurses. Check up on the sickest patient you saw yesterday. Count your blessings. Work hard. Play hard. Bring love to work. Remember that family comes before medicine in family medicine. I was only in Ontario for two weeks, but I think I learned more in those fourteen days than I did in four years "on the hill." I kept a diary of my experience, and wrote then, "Dr. Daniels is the consummate family doctor. He is so connected to his town! I admire his energy, his skill, but most of all his compassion. He is everything I would hope to be. I want to be a family physician."

Driving back from Ontario I found myself inspired in a new way – I finally knew that I had no doubt about my future. I had witnessed and experienced the epitome of a medical practitioner. Dr. Daniels was the role model I had been seeking.

He was, and remains today, a hero of my heart.

(Above printed in the Spring 2004 edition of the Oregon Family Physician)

When I stumbled on to Dave's article (printed above) about ten years after I had retired I got on the phone and called him. I said "Dave, you sure know how to make a grown man cry don't you?" His calm and unhesitating response was a simple "I meant every word of it!" I can't think of a nicer tribute.

Some Awards and Certificates

Where Medicine Might Be Headed
A Personal Opinion

For centuries there has been a special relationship between a doctor and a patient. This "Doctor-Patient" relationship has been somewhat unique. The special ingredients of this bonding phenomenon include a mixture of trust, mutual respect, and an element of true love. This is not a sexually oriented love, nor is it an infatuation like some people get with rock stars or celebrities. The relationship creates a comfort zone that allows for sharing of sensitive and personal information without fear of a loss of confidentiality.

When I started into the field of medicine in the early 1950s, the Doctor-Patient relationship was still very much intact. Patients came to doctors with their problems, the doctor treated them, and any financial arrangements were between the two parties. If the patient could not pay for the service provided something could be worked out – whether is was a token low payment, small payments over time, a barter with farm produce, an exchange of services, or something else. The arrangement remained between the doctor and the patient. Very few people had medical insurance at that time, and if they did have insurance it was usually for hospital care only. If the doctor reduced his fees for hardship the patient was very grateful and appreciative.

Gradually over time, more and more people got health insurance. Sometimes the insurance was obtained through union or employer benefit packages. Occasionally individuals would buy health insurance directly from the insurance companies to help with large unforeseen expenditures. Most early health insurance policies only covered hospitalization and the office costs were still left as the patient's responsibility. This arrangement led patients to want to be placed in the hospital for minor procedures which had usually been done in the doctor's office. Hospitals liked the increased revenues and soon the insurance companies realized that their costs could be lowered if they included out patient and office services in their contracts. Technologic advances exploded in the 1960s and 1970s vastly raising the costs of services and also prolonging life in terminal cases which made end of life care much more expensive. A new generation of specialists learned that they could keep patients alive much longer with ventilators, artificial feedings, expensive laboratory monitoring, and new medications and equipment. Some of these intensive care specialists developed an attitude that no one should be allowed to die on their shift. Hopeless cases were kept alive for weeks or months because no one was willing to "pull the plug." Lawyers had a field day entering the fray and accusing doctors of doing too much or too little, often creating rifts between families and the doctors, with the idea of making big money for themselves at someone else's expense. Some new technologies had occasional failures and again lawyers pushed the costs of service higher and higher via lawsuits, and manufacturing companies, hospitals, and doctors had to keep raising charges in order to meet rapidly rising product liability and malpractice premiums. Insurance companies who were now the payers, instead of the individuals, made lots of noise about how the medical profession was charging too much and they, the insurance companies, were doing everything they could to control costs. The cost controls were always aimed at the hospitals and the doctors who were getting squeezed more and more by the rising costs of doing business. The insurance companies and the governmental agencies that were responsible for payments to hospitals and doctors publicly condemned doctors and hospitals for being greedy. Legislators were willing to make laws to control doctors' and hospitals' fees, but were totally unwilling to address one of the very costly underlying factors of the rising costs – namely the proliferation of lawsuits. Legislative bodies usually have a high percentage of lawyers and they receive massive amounts of lobbying money from the Trial Lawyers Association so it is unlikely that they will ever arrive at a good balance of solutions.

Another factor which has degraded the Doctor-Patient relationship, other than the doctors and hospitals being labeled as greedy, is the insistence by the governmental agencies and insurance companies to label us as "providers" rather than doctors. They also insist on calling our patients "clients." I know that just changing the titles shouldn't bother me but it does. I think a little of the magic in the Doctor-Patient relationship is lost when you switch to Provider-Client.

What's ahead? I see the probability that the government will finally get its way and take over the entire health care system. The argument will be that only they can control the rising costs. What we will get with the socialized medicine will be a steady degradation in the quality of health care. Care will be limited on the basis of artificial parameters

182

as it is elsewhere where socialized health care is in place. If you are over a specific age you will be denied certain procedures because the cost will exceed your "worth" regardless of your physiologic age. Patients from Canada who are under a socialized system have been coming to the United States and paying to get care that is denied them in their own country. Do you remember the patient I had who came to see me from California? She was able to take a vacation trip and have me treat her at less cost for the package than she would incur at her home town for the treatment alone. That same principle is well established now in this mobile society where Americans and others from many other countries are going to Asia to get expensive procedures done in very modern hospitals because the cost there is so much lower where they do not have high malpractice awards and product liability costs. People have found out that they can take a nice foreign vacation trip and get their surgery done in a package deal for less cost than they can have the procedure alone done at home.

I suspect that eventually the doctors will all be salaried government employees and they might not even have a choice as to where they will live and practice. There will be no incentive to be highly productive. If a surgeon is used to doing five cases in the operating room per day now he is likely to do two or three in the socialized system – why not, he gets paid the same amount: this is the inefficient way that socialistic systems work. You are not likely to see the same doctor on repeat visits and you are likely going to be cared for by another provider – a Nurse Practitioner or a Physician's Assistant for most routine type care. I have nothing against NPs or PAs – they can do a lot to improve efficiency but there are a lot of times that the initial assessment should be done by a doctor. When you go to a clinic with a new problem you are probably going to have your first contact with a clerk who will enter information into your supposedly private computerized medical file. The clerk will then decide on the basis of some computer algorithm which provider you are to see next. This order of who sees you first and steers your initial care is totally out of touch with what has been learned in the military triage experience. In the battlefield situation (and that is not too far removed from the current emergency room scenario) the most experienced and mature physician available is the first to make the assessment because his experienced judgment factors in severity of condition, available resources, who can quickly be treated and moved out compared to the those who will require massive amounts of blood, surgical facilities, diagnostic equipment, and time. During triage, the experienced physician's assessment goal is aimed at doing the best possible job for the most people with the resources available. He will put aside for comfort treatment those too severely wounded or too ill to justify extensive use of available resources until the less critical have been treated and moved on. This may seem cruel but the reality is that if you use all of your available blood supplies and tie up all of your surgeons for an almost hopeless case you are denying help to those who would benefit the most from the most efficient utilization of resources. Contrast that to the clerk with no real medical training who will enter key words from your presenting complaint into the data base. The computer will then massage the new data and merge it with your old data and according to a protocol decide what treatments or assessments you should have and who should be your next provider. Protocols have their place and can work in many instances but computers and clerks don't have the depth of observation skills held by the experienced physician. I have treated a cowboy in his 90s who was bucked off of a horse and had a head injury that required neurosurgical intervention (removal of subdural hematoma) and was back taking care of his horses within a few weeks. The computer would quite likely have denied treatment or have delayed an MRI based on his age and the assumption that he was too old to benefit.

Confidentiality will be "guaranteed" but any person representing a governmental agency that has anything to do with funding will have ready access to your records. Any diagnosis – correct or not - will stay with you forever and may affect what treatment you are eligible for, or denied, in the future no matter where you go. Most expensive tests like MRIs will be scheduled many weeks or even months away even though treatment based on those tests may be urgent. It will appear at first that costs may be controlled but the real costs with the tremendous expansion of tax-supported governmental employees will be much higher in the long run. How much will all these services cost? Including the massive bureaucracy that will be formed the cost will be astronomical and will continue to rise. It will require higher and higher taxes in order to pay for the "free services."

In addition to the cost control factors discussed above I fear that socializing the medical services of the country will lead to some absolutely stupid, top-down, one-shoe-fits-all-type directives. I have mentioned throughout this book several incidents where non-medical persons with authority have made ridiculous medical decisions. I recall attending a national rural health conference in the 1970s where there was a big push for the highways safety act before Congress. The proposals described for the rural health aspects included having paid ambulance crews available to any highway accident within some time frame like twenty minutes. I may not have remembered the exact time requirements mentioned but I knew it was totally impractical for places like my community and the surrounding areas where we had to rely heavily on volunteer services. I finally raised my hand and told them that I was from a small town and that some of what they were talking about didn't seem to make sense. I asked them to please define what they meant by "rural." The immediate, and to me, surprising answer was – "any town of 200,000 or less." We who live in towns of 10,000 or less really don't consider cities of 200,000 to be rural. Certainly policies that might apply to a town of 200,000 might not make sense for a town of 10,000.

I recall another conference that I attended concerning plans being proposed to improve the care of newborn infants and their mothers. Based on population data they were trying to get legislation setting up maternity centers to which all deliveries were to be directed. These were to be staffed by Obstetricians and Pediatricians only. No Family Practitioners would be qualified. In our area we were very short handed in both of those specialties but all of the doctors and nurses who were involved with care of newborns took special training in resuscitation of newborns. Based on population data the only hospitals to be certified for delivery and newborn care in southwest Idaho and eastern Oregon were to be Boise, Idaho, and Pendleton and Bend, Oregon. They apparently wanted patients to travel up to a hundred and fifty miles, sometime on bad roads, for prenatal care and delivery when many had a hospital in their own town or close by. Family Practice physicians were to be excluded from participation but at the same time there was a big push to train midwives because of the shortage of obstetrical specialists. If these types of policy nightmares can be dictated by a "Health Czar" instead of being scrutinized by a somewhat thoughtful legislative process I suspect that we will have really serious problems.

Do I have all of the answers to the health care cost problem? No!
Do I have some suggestions for improving the system? Yes!

185

- Stop making the practice of medicine a lottery for lawyers. Patients still need to have legal protection against true malpractice and injury but frivolous suits and ridiculously high jury awards have driven costs way beyond reason. If lawyers and patients had some expectation of having to pay some of the legal and court costs of bringing frivolous suits they would not be as eager to make non-meritorious claims. I would also like to see realistic caps on malpractice awards and product liability awards so that judgments are more in line with reality – "actual costs incurred" and "loss of income" need to be more honestly evaluated.

- Stop the current trend of limiting doctors concerning diagnostic tests that they are allowed to order based on the patient's current list of diagnoses. If the threat of lawsuits is moderated doctors will not need to practice as much expensive "defensive medicine" but they still need to be able to confirm or deny their suspicions of medical conditions that are not already in the patient's chart. A physician nowadays has usually acquired about twelve or more years of education beyond high school and should be able to trump a clerk and a computer on deciding which tests would be in the best interest of the patient.

- Everyone needs some sort of catastrophic medical insurance. There are very few families that would not be wiped out financially in the event of a serious accident or illness such as cancer. Catastrophic insurance could be quite inexpensive if the kick in point was quite high. I generally do not like to have government involved in policies that the private sector historically has handled better, but catastrophic insurance might be one I could accept. That would make primary health insurance much more affordable for almost everyone as the insurance companies would not have to factor in the extremely costly patients. For those truly destitute perhaps some help with insurance premiums might be provided under their welfare program. However, I think that no one should have every bit of their care provided for free. There should be at least a token charge or co-pay assessment for doctor's office, urgent care clinics, and emergency room visits. When things are free the system invariably becomes overused and abused. It has been well-established that patients are more appreciative of their care and are more likely to follow instructions if they have any,

186

even a very small, out of pocket expense related to their care. Even Communist China learned that lesson and started charging token payments for health care visits. They found out that minor complaints which were bogging down and overloading their system dropped precipitously when token charges were imposed. Look at what has happened in Southern California – illegal immigrants, welfare recipients, and deadbeats so overloaded the emergency services that many of the emergency rooms had to close their doors which totally eliminated the services for everyone else. In this situation those individuals who were abusing the system knew that the whole medical delivery system was living under federal mandates that they had to provide emergency care regardless of an individual's ability to pay. (Unfunded mandates are a huge problem in many fields as well as medicine.) These people are actually instructed by their well wishers to call an ambulance to go to the emergency rooms for minor problems because "the ambulance and hospital have to take care of you for free" and if you called a cab you would have to pay. Much of what is going wrong in this country is resulting from an attitude change from self-responsibility to one of "the government must take care of me!"

- Some medical and surgical procedures should not be covered by either medical insurance or government funded health care programs. I know this will be controversial but I don't think the general public should be forced to pay, via either insurance premiums or taxes, for another person's elective vanity cosmetic procedures. Plastic surgery for reconstruction following burns and injuries is one thing but most elective face lifts and breast augmentation surgery is another. There are many other examples that could be described that should remain in the "private pay" arena. If special interest groups cry foul let them put their money where their mouth is and let them help with the costs for affected individuals, but don't ask the general public to finance procedures that the vast majority of the public do not promote.

- Try to educate the public (and admittedly a lot of the public really does not want to be educated) that a physician who must pay up to a $100,000 (some high risk specialties are more) for malpractice insurance, pay nurses and office staff perhaps another $200,000 plus office rent, electricity, phones, medical supplies etc. may not really have a high personal income at all when the office brings in $350,000 or $400,000 per year.

- We need to get this nation back on course with the principles of the Founding Fathers. Sure, a lot of the philosophy in the documents that were generated in the founding of the country was based on Christian principles but that doesn't mean that they are reserved for church services. The "do unto others" and the "thou shalt not" directives are not just religious directives but are the basis for the laws that govern us all. They protect citizens of all types and faiths and should not be discarded just because they were espoused by a religious leader. We have lost trust in our fellow man. Political activists have driven wedges of class envy and jealousies in their attempt to gain political power and control. Many politically active organizations that have great influence on our lawmakers have "one agenda" items that totally ignore the overall picture of what is good for the country. Many of our lawmakers have been in Washington for so long that they really are out of touch with the common man. Common sense seems to be something we seem to remember from some time long ago. I hope it, common sense, returns with a flourish and that our medical care system becomes less expensive and still remains compassionate and the envy of the rest of the world.

Tree and Old Building at Plush Oregon

Afterword

This book, which started out as a "few stories" for my grandchildren, has grown into my life story and includes my thoughts and observations concerning the evolution of some aspects of the practice of medicine and some thoughts on what might be ahead for medicine in this country. While writing this book I have become acutely aware that the six generations of my family that I have known - two generations older, my own generation, and three younger generations - have been a great source of strength and joy. I have been blessed.

I wish to credit several persons who have helped get this project started or completed. My grandson Mike and his wife Becky were instrumental in getting me started with their request that I provide stories for their children. My sister Miriam (Mino) who had to put up with me as a younger brother in childhood has been invaluable. We have had lots of fun reliving our childhood as she worked tirelessly to help me redirect misplaced commas and rewrite awkward sentences. Without her help I am not sure that I would have had a printable project. Margaret Russell, who at age 90 was also writing her first book, had finished her book a couple of months before I completed mine. I had encouraged her to finish her book and then she stood at the "finish line" and kept waving me in. I also wish to thank Teresa Sales of Caxton Printers for her technical support and cheerful encouragement.

For the reader who got the book primarily for my personal and family history I hope that I have not overwhelmed you with the history of medicine that I have witnessed. For the reader who used the book primarily for the history of medicine I hope that my personal biography was unique enough that you were not severely bored.

What are my future plans? I will be busy helping update and republish some local history volumes. I doubt that I will do any more writing of my own. I will continue to be active with my lifelong photographic hobby. I will try to catch up on some projects that have been ignored while I was writing this book.

Most of the photographs in the book are mine. My sister Mino contributed a few pictures (Western trip and splinter removal) and the early pictures of me and my family were taken by my folks or my brother. The picture on this page was taken by my daughter-in-law Linda.

How do I want to be remembered? Perhaps as a blessed person who did some interesting things in his lifetime, but most importantly as a physician who took good care of his patients.

Dorin S. Daniels, M.D. – retired

Doctor D - Age 80 in 2008

The Daniels Rock Group

This picture shows our entire family on a camping trip in 1987. The location is near Fish Lake in the Wallowa Mountains of Eastern Oregon. This was one of our favorite camp sites and is about a half mile from the Fish Lake Campground in a meadow on Lake Fork Creek. Highest on the rock is Alan's family – Alan at top. Randy, Brian and Mike (L-R) sitting below Alan, and Linda standing. In the middle row sitting are (L-R) De Wilda and Kathy. In the front row (L-R)) are Don's family – Terry, Jennifer, Don and Kelly. Toddy and Dorin are on the right side in the front row. Photo was done with a Canon 35mm SLR camera on a tripod, timer, and a mad dash to get into the picture.

191

This Gate is Adjacent to a Hiking Path Around the Reservoir at Evergreen, Colorado

Some pictures bring smiles and need no captions.

This Rest Stop is Quite Remote - Nevada Really Promotes Tourism - Even for Dogs

President Harry Truman on Whistle Stop Tour in Madison, Wisconsin - 1948

This poor quality picture is in the book because it is of historical and family interest. This picture was taken with a very cheap 35mm camera while President Truman was on the campaign trail and visiting Madison, Wisconsin for a speech. My cousin David Bell was his speech writer and was accompanying the President. During the President's speech at a downtown auditorium later in the day my cousin David came to our house so we could visit, catch up on family news, and listen to the speech on the radio. (We had no TVs in those days.) We were trying to visit and listen to the speech at the same time when David suddenly bristled and blurted out – "Damn, he ad-libbed that line!" referring to a comment the President had made. David was soft spoken and I had not heard him swear before so President Truman must have strayed fairly far from the script.

Can you imagine the panic the current Secret Service would have if they had to protect the President in circumstances similar to those in the above picture?

Kathy and De Wilda in Road Near Whitney Oregon Circ 1963

It helps to have daughters for photo subjects.

De Wilda Resting on Trail from Twin Lakes to Blue Hole - Wallowa Mountains 1972

Trees at Brundage Mountain Ski Area After Snowstorm

One of the great things about skiing is the constantly changing beauty of the winter landscape.

Snow Drifts On Tree Stumps - Brundage Mountain Ski Area

Alaska Snow Scene - Anchorage to Seward Highway - 1956

You probably have guessed by now that I love snow scenes. Both of these pictures were taken with Canon 35mm cameras.

Marble Canyon Sunrise on the Colorado River

If this picture looks familiar you might have seen one just like it in Arizona Highways photographed by Gary Ladd. Gary was the instructor at an Elderhostel photographic program that Toddy and I attended in February 1998. It was a cold, dreary, overcast morning and the sun broke through the clouds just at sunrise to allow this "once in a lifetime" picture. Gary used a large view camera and I used a 35mm Canon Elan II SLR with Fujichrome Sensia II film.

Cousins Jumping in Sand Dunes Near Cabin in Door County - 1965

If there is a sand dune available kids will jump. Unfortunately this dune has been replaced by a house so my great-grandchildren won't be able to jump there.

(L-R) Alan, Kathy, Don, De Wilda - Stuck in Sand - Lake Michigan at D6 Cabin - 1965

Sand, water, and kids result in infinite types of fun. None of these crazy activities were taught or planned.

D6 Cabin Reunion 1965 - All of the Three Generations Are Present

F jr   Marty   Dorin   Alice   Jim
FD Sr OBD Mino Betsey Toddy Jon Florence
George   Alan   Don   Jane
Chris David Sarah De Wilda Kathy Ann

Farrington Daniels, Sr (1889-1972) m. Olive Bell (1891–1984)
Farrington Daniels Jr (1918–2002) m. Alice Monroe (1920 -)
    Betsey (1952 -), George (1953-), Chris (1957 – 2006)
Florence Daniels (1920-) m. Jim Drury (1918-)
    Jon (1948-), Jane (1952-), Ann (1957-)
Miriam (Mino) Daniels (1924-) m. Marty Ludwig (1926–)
    David (1957-), Sarah (1959-)
Dorin Daniels (1927-) m. Kathryn (Toddy) Meyer (1926 - 2003)
    Don (1952-), Alan (1953-), Kathy (1956-), De Wilda (1959-)

Most didn't want to dress up for the picture but Grandma insisted. It was quite uncommon to get everyone together at one time. I don't know who took the picture but I suspect my brother set it up with a timer or a neighbor.

Shanghai 2005

These pictures were taken in 2005 with a 4 mega pixel Canon Digital Elph. They do not represent modern China well but I thought the Fast Food establishment and the Movie Poster showed an interesting, and humorous, culture mix.

Haystack Rock at Canon Beach - Northern Oregon Coast

The picture above, taken from Ecola State Park, was on a stormy day and the sun broke through the clouds at just the right time. Both pictures were taken with Canon SLR film cameras.

Gulls on Posts - Olympic Peninsula - Washington State

Alvord Ranch Barn at Steens Mountain - SE Oregon

The above picture is on the east side of the Steens Mountain in S.E Oregon and the bottom picture is on the western slope of Steens Mountain at Fish Lake.

Steens Mountain at Fish Lake - S.E. Oregon

Sugarloaf Mountain - North Side - Eagle Cap Wilderness - Eastern Oregon

Sugarloaf Mountain in the Eagle Cap Wilderness of Eastern Oregon was one of our favorite hiking destinations. We hiked there for many years from our camping location near Fish Lake. Unfortunately some of the area has been devastated by forest fires.

Sugarloaf Mountain - South Side - Eagle Cap Wilderness - Eastern Oregon

Lake Powell - 1999 Elderhostel Photo Expedition

The above Lake Powell picture was taken with a tripod, close to the ground, wide angle lens, and small aperture for maximum depth of field. The sunsets at Lake Powell are spectacular and the colors change by the minute.

Lake Powell at Sunset - Elderhostel Photography Course - 1999

East Eagle Creek - Wallowa Mountains - Eastern Oregon

The above picture is near where "Paint Your Wagon" was filmed. It was taken one-handed while riding a horse.

Wild Sheep Near Durkee, Oregon

Alvord Ranch Cattle - East of Steens Mountain in S.E. Oregon

I love taking mountain pictures.

Maroon Bells near Aspen Colorado